21st-Century Man—Emerging

21st-
Century
Man—

Emerging

Clyde Reid

A Pilgrim Press Book
Philadelphia

901.9
R353 t

Contents

To my mother . . .
who wanted me to be a doctor,
and my dad . . .
who wanted me to be a businessman,
for allowing me the freedom to be myself.

Preface

Something beautiful and exciting is happening! A new species of man is being born in our midst. A new man who is more free to be himself and to be real. A man *and a woman* who are more authentic and more open, yet more responsible to themselves and their world.

This book is a joyous announcement of that fact. I believe it to be a fact, and I have pulled together some of the clues that have convinced me it is really happening.

I'm not sure when this conviction first seized me, but after it did, I found supporting evidence on every hand. I first presented the idea in public when asked to address the Toledo Clergy Association in the spring of 1968. The response, which was basically positive, encouraged me that I was on the right track. I have since tested the idea of the new man with many people at retreats and workshops, and have consistently met with enthusiastic responses together with some skepticism.

I am grateful to the Cincinnati Monthly Meeting of the Religious Society of Friends for inviting me to be their Shared Ministry Lecturer in October 1969, an occasion which helped me polish some of my thought on the new man. The assembled clergy of the Swedenborgian Church in America also gave me valuable feedback on the new-man concept at their national assembly in Windsor, Ontario, in 1969.

My appreciation is also due some of the leaders of the

human potential movement with whom I have studied, and who have helped me discover the new man seeking expression in myself. I think especially of Claudio Naranjo, Charlotte Selver and Charles Brooks.

There have also been countless friends who have encouraged me in the writing of this book, not only by their words but by showing me the new man in themselves. Jerry and Marilyn Kerns have opened their home and hearts to me, and it is at their desk that the final touches were done to this manuscript. Willis Elliott, one of our great minds, supported my conviction in the new man, and likewise shared his home with me. In his study, portions of two of my books were written. Mike Murphy, president of the Esalen Institute, shared his conviction that I was on the right track.

Other friends have done far more than they realize by their enthusiasm and encouragement: Peg Rouse, Jerry Jud, Don Kelly, Sharon Klaus, Sarah Williams, Kathleen Cosgrove. Their warmth floods the pages of this book.

Patricia Hyatt, who typed the manuscript and made many helpful suggestions, and Nancy Mestrovic, who assisted her, deserve my warm gratitude.

Clyde H. Reid

Columbus, Indiana

The
New
Man

The single, stunning, enormous fact of our times is that psycho-social man is undergoing a mutation; he is making the "Great Psychic Leap."

We tend to think of mutations as being biological and of occurring purely in the genetic structure or process, have it as you will, of germ plasm. This is because the terminology originated with the geneticists. But social organisms undergo mutations too, and that is what we are talking about here.

There may be a new species of man emerging, and he may create a wholly new society, a new science, a new philosophy, a new religion, and a new morality. The mutational force is his own technology; the hard rays of his own making have created within the social organism the necessity for a change of truly universal dimensions.[1]

Don Fabun

There is a new man walking the earth today.

He is like a halo which follows the old man around
   seeming to disappear at times
   yet coming again and again
      sometimes faintly
      and sometimes with great clarity.

And on occasion, that halo
   that shadow of the new man
   takes on flesh
   while the old man fades away.

I   really   deeply   earnestly   believe
      there is a new man emerging in our midst today.
A new species of human being
An evolutionary leap
A new type of person
      who is more free and yet more responsible
      who is more open and more aware
      a world citizen, a universal man, a man of peace.
The new man is both old and new.
He has his roots in history.
He has appeared here and there, now and then.
   We can see him in
      Moses
      and Isaiah,

in Gotama Buddha
and Gandhi.
We can see him in
Jesus of Nazareth
and Socrates,
in St. Francis
and Martin Luther.

And yet today he is emerging in a new way, with a new boldness and a new urgency. We find him in every culture, every race. He is emerging because he must, because God is calling him out of the cocoon of his infancy into the freedom of his adolescence. He is emerging in all of us.

Who is the new man?
The new man is a Roman Catholic nun in a short skirt, a pretty blouse, and a lovely hairdo . . . dancing for joy.

The new man is a sixteen-year-old boy explaining the civil rights movement to his father.

The new man is Martin Luther King, Jr. Alexander Dubcek. Bobbie Kennedy. Benjamin Spock.

The new man is Corita Kent and Margaret Mead.

The emergence of the new man is good news! He comes as a sign of hope and cause for joy. I feel joy in the depths of my being as I say this.

There is much in the news today that brings sadness and is cause for despair.
War continues and war threatens
Human atrocities are committed, denied, forgotten
Young people are caught by the drug scene
Old people take money to permit the drug scene

Millions continue to live in subhuman housing
   with subhuman incomes
   eating subhuman food
   chasing subhuman rats
   across their children's beds.
There is gloom enough
     but there is *also* HOPE in the world today,
        and
 the   new   man   is   a   sign   of   hope!
      Thank   God
      the
      new
      man
      is
      coming,
he is in process of becoming and is here in our midst
   all at the same time.

  I hope you will
     recognize the new man
     accept the new man
     rejoice in the new man
       and
     become the new man!

Note to The New Man

1   Don Fabun, *The Dynamics of Change* (Englewood Cliffs, N.J.: Prentice-Hall, 1967), p. 26.

14

Characteristics of the New Man

I am fascinated these days by what I am convinced is a most significant phenomenon. I am seeing a New Man emerging. I believe this New Man is the person of tomorrow. I want to talk about him.

I have seen him emerging, partially formed, from encounter groups, sensitivity training, so-called T-groups. I realize that for many years I saw facets of him emerging in the deep relationship of individual psychotherapy. I see him showing his face in the rapidly growing trend toward a humanistic and human psychology. I see him in the new type of student emerging on our campuses, and in campus unrest all over the world. . . . He is not all lovable, but he is emerging.

Carl R. Rogers, unpublished speech
"The Person of Tomorrow"

Introduction

If there really is a new man emerging in our midst, who is he? What is he like and where may he be found?

In the passages that follow, I am going to suggest twelve characteristics of the new man that help me recognize him when I see him.

I want to warn at the outset against identifying the new man as any one group or type. To say that the hippie is the new man is too simple, although some hippies are beautiful people and express dimensions of the new man. To say that youth today represent the new man is too simple, although many young people exhibit these qualities. So do some of our elders.

The emergence of the new man is more subtle than that. The new man is in you—to some extent. The new man is in me—to some extent. The new man is in all of us—in some degree. Some of us are more frightened of him and suppress him or deny him or murder him when we become aware of his presence in us. Others have more freedom to admit the emergence of the new man in them and let him out, permit his expression.

I think this is really the meaning of the term "up-tight" which is in such vogue today. The up-tight person tightens up because he senses the conflict within himself between the old man and the new. If he is really content to be rigid and moralistic and judgmental, he has no conflict. It is when he encounters the new man in another person and recog-

I would totally agree with you that a new type of human being is emerging today, not just the collective tribal man emerging out of a global convergence of mankind, but also in many ways a totally new type of human being. Since man has taken into his own hands the direction, pace, and depth of his own biological and psychological evolution, we can in fact now create man in any image we choose. In Genesis, God created man in his own image, but now man shares in that ongoing creation to make man in his own image, as *we* choose.[1]

Robert T. Francoeur, Ph.D.

There are an almost infinite number of ways to differentiate between the old and new cultures. The old culture, when forced to choose, tends to give preference to property rights over personal rights, technological requirements over human needs, competition over cooperation, violence over sexuality, concentration over distribution, the producer over the consumer, means over ends, secrecy over openness, social reforms over personal expression, striving over gratification, Oedipal love over communal love, and so on. The new counterculture tends to reverse all of these priorities.[2]

Philip E. Slater

nizes deeply that the new man is also in him that he tightens up—out of fear—to keep the new man in him from popping out and rocking the boat. It is when we see ourselves in others that we become anxious.

The search for the new man is a very personal thing for me. I know the new man because I know him in myself. I am not the same person I was five years ago, or ten years ago. I am myself more free and more open and more responsible. There is a constant tension within me between the man who wants to be free and open and joyous, and the norms and expectations of my culture, my country, my job, my profession, my religion. I must constantly weigh whether these norms and expectations are still valid, still responsible, or whether they have become rigid and outmoded, limiting freedom and killing the spirit within me.

I also feel more open to new truth, new ways of seeing reality, new ways of doing things. I now recognize the validity of Eastern meditation, Roman Catholic piety, pentecostal fervor, where before I dismissed them more easily on some intellectual pretext. I feel a new kinship with nature, a deeper oneness with men of all sorts, a more vital connection with my own senses. I have changed in many ways, and I see these changes in people all around me.

I recently spoke about the new man to a church group, and afterward I was talking to the minister. I asked him, "Do you believe it?" He exclaimed, "I *know* it's true, because I feel it in myself!" I have had this response from enough people all over the country to convince me that there is something basically true in my claim. I have found affirmation from Ph.D.'s and farmers alike, from clergy and laity, men and women, young and old.

On many occasions, when I have spoken about the new man, I have asked for a nonverbal response to the idea. I pass out sheets of paper and crayons and ask people to respond with color and shape and symbol. I urge them to respond with negative feelings as well as positive. While I have found some skepticism or resistance to the idea, the most prominent reaction was an expression of joy and recognition. Some beautiful explosions of color and light bursting forth in these drawings helped convince me that the average man can find within himself the reality of this truth.

There is nothing sacred about the twelve characteristics I have chosen to elaborate. You may want to add some others, or rename some of mine. They are simply handles which help me to make some sense of this exciting phenomenon of the new man. I may have a different list by tomorrow morning.

One obvious characteristic of twentieth-century man which I have not elaborated upon, is the fact that he is increasingly technological man. I have been asking myself why I have not included this as one of my twelve hallmarks of the new man. Perhaps it is because I feel the new man is a response to technological man, a corrective to the dehumanizing tendencies of modern technology. I do not mean to imply that man will be less technological. That would be a foolish claim indeed, as we can daily observe ourselves becoming more and more dependent upon the mechanical hardware of our century. I am trying to describe the more deeply human qualities which can allow us to live with our technology in a more satisfying way rather than being automatized along with our possessions. It is the new man emerging which will help us escape the Orwellian 1984.

It is one of my observations that we can find present in our culture caricatures of each of these twelve qualities. We find people who are living overstatements of one dimension of the new man, as if to call our attention dramatically to the importance of that reality. Some hippies may be incarnations of freedom in the extreme. Some people become so wrapped up in man's psychic dimension that they neglect their relationships in this life. Some drug-high individuals may be overstatements of the new "turned-on" man, the aware man. While we may be horrified at some of these "overstatements" when we meet them in the flesh, there is validity in trying to understand the truth behind the over-statement. Some of those we reject so easily are perhaps necessary pioneers, exploring the frontiers of man's nature so we may more comfortably follow.

If there is a new man emerging, then that fact has deep implications for all of us. How do we communicate with the new man? How must the structures of our society change to accommodate the new man? I will explore some of these implications in my concluding essay. First, let us examine the characteristics of the new man in more detail.

Notes to Introduction of Characteristics of the New Man

1   Robert T. Francoeur, Ph.D., biologist and author of *Man and Evolution,* from a personal letter.
2   Philip E. Slater, "Cultures in Collision," *Psychology Today,* July 1970, p. 31.

Strangely enough, I would turn to the Almighty and say, "If you allow me to live just a few years in the second half of the twentieth century, I will be happy." Now that's a strange statement to make because the world is all messed up, the nation is sick, trouble is in the land, confusion all around . . . that's a strange statement. But I know somehow that only when it is dark enough can you see the stars. And I see God working in this period of the twentieth century in a way that men in some strange way are responding. Something is happening in our world. The masses of people are rising up, whether they are in Johannesburg, South Africa, Nairobi, Kenya, Ghana, New York City, Atlanta, Georgia, Jackson, Mississippi, or Memphis, Tennessee, the cry is always the same, "We want to be free."[1]

Martin Luther King, Jr.

This is the revolution of the new generation. Their protest and rebellion, their culture, clothes, music, drugs, ways of thought, and liberated life-style are not a passing fad or a form of dissent and refusal, nor are they in any sense irrational. The whole emerging pattern, from ideals to campus demonstrations to beads and bell bottoms to the Woodstock Festival, makes sense and is part of a consistent philosophy. It is both necessary and inevitable, and in time it will include not only youth, but all people in America. . . .

At the heart of everything is what we shall call a change of consciousness. This means a "new head"— a new way of living—a new man. This is what the new generation has been searching for, and what it has started achieving.[2]

Charles A. Reich

Free
Man

I stepped off the KLM jet at Schiphol Airport in Amsterdam, made my way through customs, and looked for Henk. As he had written, he was easy to spot in a crowd. He stood six feet four inches, with a magnificent flowing beard and bushy hair. I saw a face that spoke of depth and understanding—and, yes, gentleness. His casual turtleneck shirt fit his easygoing manner. His voice was firm and rich—a voice with authority.

We walked to his car, exchanging thoughts and feeling a rare bond of friendship grow between us. He was a relaxed, jovial man who was able to listen, to be really present for another.

We ate lunch beside a canal drawbridge, in a delightful restaurant that had been a blacksmith's shop in Henk's youth. As we ate, Henk spoke of the exciting work he was doing in adult education, involving people in creative play as a learning experience. He spoke with great excitement and enthusiasm as he described the use of pantomime, collage, mask-making, and other creative educational methods. His eyes sparkled as he spoke of lives he had seen changed.

In Europe, Henk is a pioneer. Few educators dare to depart from the traditional approaches to experiment in educational methods as Henk and his colleagues are doing.

The more I saw of Henk throughout that day, the more I felt the presence of a free man. Trained as a minister, he was sufficiently free of old forms and methods to experiment

a professor at the University of Minnesota who teaches a class in "Human Sexual Behavior." In order to help his students speak freely and without embarrassment about sexual matters, he has them repeat out loud some of the vocabulary. Each student in the classroom is instructed to turn to someone sitting beside him and repeat words like "sexual intercourse." If they seem shy about it, the professor says, "Louder." He explains, "This idea that sex talk is dirty talk is deeply ingrained in us. I have to desensitize my students so that sexuality becomes less loaded for them. Saying the words out loud is a good start."[3]

I have observed an increasing freedom among people to speak openly and frankly about matters which would have been considered terribly embarrassing a few years ago. The new man is learning to be free in his use of language.

The new man is becoming more free in his dress, too. I remember a conversation with a friend who is an automobile executive. He explained to me that no executive working in his research division would dare to wear anything but a dark suit and tie to work. If he wore even a *conservative* sport coat, he would be in danger of being regarded as eccentric.

While the influence of mass culture may still be stamping out stereotyped persons, there are heartening countertrends. I attended a fashionable suburban church one Sunday to find the minister leading worship in a short-sleeved turtleneck sport shirt, looking very cool and refreshed. I passed a minister's wife recently who was wearing a bright red leatherette miniskirt, hardly expressing the old image of a lady churchmouse. (I'm not suggesting that all ministers' wives should try miniskirts!) My point is that there seems to be increasing freedom on the part of both men and women to wear bright, comfortable clothing with a great deal of individuality. This does not deny that we still see much conformity to the fashion dictates of mass media advertising and the fashion industry.

An encouraging sign of the new freedom in dress has been the revolt of many women against the midiskirt. When fashion designers lowered skirts to mid-calf for the fall 1970 fashions, masses of women refused to go along. Everywhere there were reports that stores which stocked up on midi-length dresses were having trouble selling them. I happened to catch a humorous radio broadcast recently purporting to be from fashion headquarters in New York. The chairman has just received a telephone message from one of his agents on Fifth Avenue: "What's that? Saks Fifth Avenue has just sold one midiskirt? Another customer is browsing in the midi department? You see, the tide is turning!" Many women turned to slack suits or continued to wear miniskirts despite the pressure from mass media. In several cities around the world, including Detroit and Mexico City, women staged public rallies protesting the long skirts and demonstrated their ire by cutting a volunteer's midiskirt to miniskirt length before a cheering crowd.

The new free man is also free in his thought. He is less fearful of challenging the orthodoxy of his parents and his elders. It now seems almost commonplace to hear of a man like the late Bishop James Pike announcing his rejection of the doctrine of the Trinity or a Thomas Altizer proclaiming that God is dead. The new man claims his right to more freedom and is granted more freedom by his peers.

This new freedom to challenge orthodoxy extends to every dimension of modern life, from religion to sexual mores to politics and patriotism. A senior high youth put it this way: "My generation . . . we say 'show me.' I don't like to take everything for granted just because people say that's the way it should be. I don't like to respect people just because other people say, you know, we should respect them."

Man's behavior is the real test, of course. It may be easy enough to feel free, to dress in a free way, or to talk more freely. I saw the new man not long ago in a church basement. I saw Negro and white teenagers dancing to the beat of Herb Alpert's Tijuana Brass—together with some of their parents and other adults of the church! It was the first time some of the adults had ever tried responding bodily to music that was not a prescribed dance step. Perhaps the real swinger of the group was a seventy-year-old retired man who danced to the rock music with the best of the youth.

After the evening ended, one of the adults said, "Now I understand for the first time what these kids are doing when they dance. They're *feeling* the music and responding with their whole bodies! It never made sense until I began to feel the music myself. I always heard it as noise, but now I can feel the beat." Something new and exciting is happening when seventy-year-olds and seventeen-year-olds can dance together for joy and understand each other more deeply as a result.

The state convention of a major religious denomination was droning on and on through a series of boring deliberations. This in itself was not remarkable, as it seems to be the custom for religious groups to spend much time in boring deliberations. One brash young minister finally became so impatient that he passed the hat among some colleagues and went next door where the Shrine Circus was playing. Armed with $30 cash, he hired three clowns and returned to the ecclesiastical proceedings. The clowns soon appeared on stage and proceeded to enliven the occasion considerably! There is a new spirit stirring today.

A junior in high school attended a workshop I led not long ago. She told us that she belonged to a high school group dedicated to support the ROTC, but that she had begun to doubt her motives for belonging to the group. She admitted that she belonged in order to be liked and approved, though deep in her conscience she had doubts about supporting the ROTC. Her parents and close friends approved of her belonging and praised her for her patriotism. As she began to explore her freedom to be honest and to be independent, she became increasingly doubtful about continuing as a member.

The new freedom seems primarily a freedom to be honest, to act on the basis of one's own conscience and one's own judgment rather than accepting the authority of others blindly. Young people seem more free to make their own vocational decisions rather than following automatically what their parents want them to become. I shall never forget the anger of an undertaker whose son preferred to be a scientist. "Why have I worked myself nearly to death to build up this business for him?" the man complained. "I've wasted years of my life, and does he appreciate it?"

In many quiet, subtle ways the new man is proclaiming that he is a free man. We see him in the changing sexual morality, we see him in the quiet way Roman Catholics ignore their Pope on the issue of birth control, we see him in the confident, strong faces of our youth, and in the freedom of the Negro to tell the white man to go to hell. The new man is proclaiming his freedom from rigid orthodoxy, from unchanging codes of behavior, and from stifling decisions made for him by other people.

The new man emerging today is more free to risk and disclose himself to others. He is more open, more known, more knowable. He knows that this freedom belongs to him and has always belonged to him. The difference is that the new man is learning how to claim that freedom which has been his all along.

Notes to 1) Free Man

1 From Dr. King's last recorded address in Memphis, Tennessee, April 3, 1968. *Renewal*, April 1969, p. 3.
2 Charles A. Reich, *The Greening of America* (New York: Random House, 1970), pp. 4–5.
3 *Look*, April 1, 1969, p. 39. Interview of Prof. Gerhard Neubeck by Nancy Gay Faber.

There are those in my generation who, somewhat wishfully, say that the kinds of commitments I have described are but a passing fancy and that, as twenty passes through thirty and into forty, with wife and child to provide for, material realities will become the prime philosophical mover. I think not, and, if I were a politician, I would not bet my future on it, for I believe we are witnessing the birth of a new kind of man who, more than his forebears, will care about the quality of life not just for himself and his family but for all men.[1]

Franklin D. Murphy

It comes down to the issue of responsibility—responding in a way to what has been done for me. In theological terms it's the thankful creature responding to the creation. This world is here and, thank God, I didn't do a thing about it to inherit it or make it, create it or anything. It's a gift and I've got to do something—without being compulsive—just in thanksgiving. This means responding in terms of other human beings, who call upon me, make claims upon my life. And these claims are social and personal.[2]

Howard Moody

Responsible Man

2

One of the most encouraging aspects of the new man emerging is that he is not simply a free man. He combines freedom with responsibility. To be free is not enough. Rugged individualism sounds romantic, but freedom untempered by responsibility becomes selfish and ultimately lonely. Certainly there are many today who have declared their freedom and opted out of society. If we asked him, the new man might put it like this:

I believe in speaking out when I feel something is wrong with this world. I want to be free of the evils of the past, but I also believe I can do something about it. I can help influence Supreme Court nominations, anti-pollution legislation and I can help with poverty programs. It isn't enough anymore to save myself if my brother goes under due to my neglect. I am my brother's keeper, and he is mine.

What encourages me is the increase in those who say, "What can I do to change things?" I heard a young housewife a few days ago say, "I'm really fired up about the pollution problem. Do any of you know of a group around here which is doing something about it? I'd like to find some people who want to work on it." On the American scene, this new responsible-free man may have been symbolized by Martin Luther King, Jr. King did not simply preach about injustice and denounce racism. He offered his time, his energy, and his talent and finally his life to do something about racism. He declared his freedom (the title of his first book was *Stride Toward Freedom*) from restrictive racial patterns, but did not "cop out" by fleeing or finding a more comfortable place for himself. He followed his convictions with responsible action.

Sen. Eugene McCarthy illustrated this dimension of the new man when he risked his political career by running in the New Hampshire primary for president in 1968. He not only declared his opposition to this nation's Vietnam policies, but followed his conviction with an earnest and responsible effort to change those policies.

Another important feature of the 1968 election campaign was the emergence of responsible youth participation. *Youth* magazine later summed it up:

This year a group of young people have changed the course of American history. The 1968 election campaign will long be remembered for those young, enthusiastic "Come-Clean-with-Gene" supporters of Senator McCarthy who forced the decision of President Johnson to step aside after that surprising New Hampshire primary. In the months that followed, the continued effort of these high school and college youth built up and carried the Minnesota senator to a nation-wide popularity that probably awed even the senator himself.

Despite the effort of some critics to minimize the importance of their work or to lump them in the same category as the young anarchists, the protestors, or the hippies, these young people may well have given impetus to a new movement of responsible youth working within The Establishment to change it.[3]

Responsible man may also be seen in a recent announcement that the President has renounced the use of germ weapons and chemical warfare agents and has banned their use by United States armed forces. While we may feel such action is long overdue, at least it is now a matter of public record. Inch by inch we are moving toward a more human society.

The new man says, "I have a responsibility to myself, to honor myself, and to grant myself the freedom I need to be a real person. But I also have to remember that my freedom impinges on my relationships with many other people. I owe them something, too."

In the fall of 1969, a new television series, "Then Came Bronson" was introduced. By the time this book is published, Bronson will probably have been replaced by a program of lower quality. It seems too good to be allowed to continue; the excellence of a program usually seems to doom it on American television.

Bronson is a young man who could be described as a drifter. He rides his motorcycle through the American countryside, and each episode portrays Bronson's experiences and relationships in a new setting. In many ways, he is the epitome of the new free man. He always seems to find enough money to live simply but satisfactorily. He breezes along the Big Sur coast in California on his motorcycle, feeling the wind in his face, stops when he wants to stop, is aware of beauty when he finds it, is envied by the automobile driver who stops alongside him and asks where he is going.

Bronson's freedom is not simply physical. He is portrayed as a person who is free to enter into deep but temporary relationships with those he encounters. He knows how to "celebrate the temporary." But he also demonstrates maturity and responsibility in his relationships. He does not exploit people. He is interested in them, cares about them, becomes involved in their pain, stays long enough to help them through a crisis. Bronson feels with people and for people.

The script also implies, though it does not become explicit, that Bronson occasionally makes love with a woman he meets and likes. He also is sensitive to the woman's life situation, and does not intrude himself into her life when she has an ongoing relationship with a husband or another man. He does not make promises he does not intend to keep. Bronson, portrayed by Michael Parks, is a sensitive, free-responsible man, and typifies some of the more attractive qualities of the new man emerging.

The sexual freedom which Bronson claims as his right is being claimed by many people today, particularly our youth. A great many adults, especially parents, are very upset about this new freedom, fearing that their youth are becoming promiscuous. Dr. Joyce Brothers, a psychologist who writes a syndicated newspaper column, discussed this issue very frankly in a story headlined: "Today's Youth: More Honest? Promiscuous? Responsible?"[4]

Dr. Brothers does not find today's youth unwholesomely preoccupied with sex. She does acknowledge that today's adolescents reach sexual maturity at an earlier age, and that there is growing recognition of female sexuality which is involved with the emerging equality of the sexes. But Dr. Brothers affirms what I have long felt—that young people are assuming increasing responsibility for establishing their own moral codes, and they are unhappy with old codes which preach one standard and secretly condone another.

With the advent of the birth control pill and other contraceptive methods, it is a fact that many people are claiming more sexual freedom for themselves. It is also true that many use that freedom irresponsibly and selfishly and foolishly, hurting themselves and others in the process. So what's new? The new and encouraging dimension is the increase of responsible decision-making on the part of many youth today. I recall the high school teacher I spoke with recently who affirmed my conviction that youth today are developing sexual responsibility. "We never had the freedom to be responsible with." And a female character in a recent television drama put it this way, "We got gypped, you know that? Our generation. Rules and regulations, that's all *we* got." She was expressing her envy of those who now have the freedom to enjoy life more—and more responsibility. If one has no freedom, he can't really be responsible. He can only be obedient or disobedient.

Notes to 2) Responsible Man

1 Franklin D. Murphy, "Yardsticks for a New Era," *Saturday Review,* November 21, 1970, p. 24.
2 From an interview by L. I. Stell in *Tempo,* November 1, 1969.
3 *Youth,* October 20, 1968, pp. 2–3.
4 *Detroit News,* December 27, 1968, p. 15A.

This continued preoccupation with money and power, no matter what the cost in humanity, has turned the young against their elders; they have discerned the hollowness of loudly proclaimed values and the shifting sands of integrity. Today's college students have returned to the ideals of our nation's earliest great citizens. These are the ideals which have been preached to them, but never practiced. To maintain his own self-respect, the idealistic youth can do no less than demand a change of direction in the university's conduct of its affairs; this the university must do if it is to maintain the respect of its students.[1]

Mrs. May O. Mastronardo

For better or worse, most of what is presently happening that is new, provocative, and engaging in politics, education, the arts, social relations (love, courtship, family, community), is the creation either of youth who are profoundly, even fanatically, alienated from the parental generation, or of those who address themselves primarily to the young.[2]

Theodore Roszak

3

Authentic Man

My dictionary speaks of "authentic" as meaning "genuine, real, trustworthy, and credible." The new man comes through as a more authentic person, real and believable, because he is in touch with his real feelings and communicates them more directly. The phony person is one who is out of touch with his real feelings, or is afraid to admit them to consciousness, or fears the consequences if he does. As a result, he communicates inauthentically. The listener knows there is something wrong, something missing, some contradiction in what he hears, something unreal, untrustworthy, or incredible.

Furthermore, the new man is unafraid to be honest about it when he hears phoniness. He is like the American Indian in North Dakota who attended a church service led by a friend of mine. Tall, impressive, and quiet, he sat in the middle of a row down near the front of the church and stolidly listened for about the first ten minutes of a very dry sermon. Suddenly he stood up and said in a loud voice, "I've stood all I could!" And slowly, with great dignity, he made his way out of the pew, up the aisle, and out the door. This kind of honesty and directness may be disturbing and may even be seen as rudeness, but *it is authentic!* The new man has begun to prize honesty above politeness, and we are often shocked by his authentic defiance of police, officials, and judges because we still prefer decorum to honesty.

If the new man had a face and a voice, he might put it this way:

> I'm not afraid to know myself. I can face the good and the bad in me and admit that all of it is me. Sure, it's scary sometimes, but it's more scary to live out some kind of phony existence. I object to those who hide behind their self-righteous masks and will not be honest with me. I want to be a whole man who is both good and bad and who can admit to both in himself.

The new man is able to admit that he has both tenderness and anger within him, both joy and pain. The old man tries to deny the stronger feelings and filter them so they come out controlled and polite and manageable. The anger he does not admit to himself or share honestly with those who deserve it builds up within him and either gets displaced on the wrong persons or tears him up inside. The new man is beginning to understand that it is all right to feel anger at times, that it is inevitable and appropriate. He also understands that it is all right to feel affection and tenderness and to express it at the appropriate times without being seen as weak. The old man is like the familiar cartoon figure who shouts "I am not angry" while he pounds his fist on the table, purple-faced with rage. He is out of touch with himself, inauthentic.

The new man knows that he is imperfect and that he is not destroyed but honored when he can admit his imperfection. The new man knows that he does not have all the answers—to anything. Furthermore, he knows that anyone who claims to have all the answers is a fool and a phony. To be sure, there are still many people running around looking for a messiah who has the complete answer to all of life's problems and questions. And there are plenty of phonies (some well-meaning phonies among them), evangelists and crusaders ready to offer people the total-truth package which will solve all their problems and answer all their questions. The sad moment is when the faithful discover the chink in their savior's armor and his infallibility bursts like a balloon. The new man does not look for any leader or any system to be perfect. He knows his own imperfection and knows that it is folly to expect perfection in someone else. Those to whom he turns for leadership are those who can be authentic and open, not those who dishonestly claim to have all the answers.

Much of the credit for this wave of authenticity in the world must be given to the psychological sciences. Psychiatry, beginning at least with Freud, has long insisted on honesty. "What do you really feel?" is the hallmark question of psychiatry, and it has almost become the hallmark question of human existence. Psychiatry has long helped people to recognize the contradiction between their words and their deeds and to own up to the conflicts. It has helped us recognize our strongest feelings and still be able to say, "All right, that's me. Those feelings of rage and sexual desire and pain are in me and I'm still a worthwhile, acceptable, lovable human being."

While psychiatry has been performing this service for the person upset enough to seek help, sensitivity training has arisen out of a universal hunger for honesty in relationships among the general population. The term "sensitivity training" as it is currently being used, calls up a wide variety of images and we are often uncertain what we mean when we use the word. Many people are attacking sensitivity training today without even knowing what they are attacking. It has become the target of reactionaries who must find something to attack. So this month they attack sex education, communism, and sensitivity training. Next month it will be motherhood, geography, and band-aids.

The sensitivity training group, as developed by some of America's leading social scientists since 1947, has been a tremendous resource for authenticity. In such groups and many varieties of small group experiences that have emerged since, a primary tool is that of personal feedback. Members of the group share with you how you come through to them. You then have a chance to compare your own view of yourself with the views of others. If you come through as inauthentic or out of touch with your feelings, the group will probably let you know this important information so you can struggle with it. I have personally found this a tremendously enlightening and valuable growth experience.

While there are some unqualified leaders who are offering "sensitivity training" experiences, when they are under qualified leadership they can be of great personal value. A recent article in *Look* magazine was entitled, "New Era in Industry: It's OK to Cry in the Office."[3] The article describes how one growing California aerospace corporation, TRW Systems Group, has utilized sensitivity training for its personnel since 1963. The president of the corporation said that he

could not afford to let creative people act defensive, sly, and touchy with each other. What if the antenna engineer hit a snag in his calculations but refused to confess the trouble for fear that it would damage his reputation and chances for promotion? What if he spent a lot of energy defending a mistake once it came to light? What if he felt resentment toward a colleague who offered help? Obviously, the man would suffer. So would the company.

The *Look* article goes on: "But the competitive culture of most organizations teaches just that sort of behavior. Human hang-ups not only make people miserable; they contaminate the work." TRW and many other corporations feel that sensitivity training, together with many other tools, can help people in their organizations be more authentic and open with each other.

In an interesting book entitled *The Ultimate Revolution,* Walter Starcke has written of his conviction that "fear-filled man" is beginning to disappear:

I can see proof of the departure of paranoia in our young people. So many of the young I have come to know take paranoia out in the open and look right at it. They have an amazing ability to smell out dishonesty. They won't brush it under the rug or let themselves be poisoned by it just because dishonesty is built into a system or is unintentional. The young refuse to live with paranoia. They refuse to put down natural man. They know that fear and evil are not natural states of man but rather are his conditions when he is not acting out of his full humanity. The young demand that life and man present wholeness.[4]

The new man is learning authenticity.

Notes to 3) Authentic Man

1 Letters to the Editor, *Saturday Review,* July 5, 1969,
   p. 19.
2 Theodore Roszak, *The Making of a Counter Culture*
   (Garden City: Anchor Books, 1969), p. 1.
3 *Look,* July 9, 1968.
4 Walter Starcke, *The Ultimate Revolution* (New York:
   Harper & Row, 1969), p. 21.

Personally, I have a great faith in the resiliency and adaptability of man, and I tend to look to our tomorrows with a surge of excitement and hope. I feel that we're standing on the threshold of a liberating and exhilarating world in which the human tribe can become truly one family and man's consciousness can be freed from the shackles of mechanical culture and enabled to roam the cosmos. I have a deep and abiding belief in man's potential to grow and learn, to plumb the depths of his own being and to learn the secret songs that orchestrate the universe. We live in a transitional era of profound pain and tragic identity quest, but the agony of our age is the labor pain of rebirth.

I expect to see the coming decades transform the planet into an art form; the new man, linked in a cosmic harmony that transcends time and space, will sensuously caress and mold and pattern every facet of the terrestrial artifact as if it were a work of art, and man himself will become an organic art form.[1]

Marshall McLuhan

4

Open
Man

If the old man has been narrow, rigid, prejudiced, war-like, nationalistic, prudish, and resistant to change, the new man is trying to be open to new ideas, new ways of relating to people and nations, new experiences, and new behavior.

The January 13, 1970 issue of *Look* magazine was devoted to a special issue of the 70's. The new man may be glimpsed here and there, may be sensed and felt in the pages of this remarkable issue. Man's new awareness that he is trying to break out of something, finds expression in these words by William Hedgepeth:

Up, Quick, if you can. It's long past time to go. You've stayed so long you've lost yourself and now exist cut off from all of you that's human. You're civilized beyond your senses: out of touch, narcotized, mechanized, Westernized, with bleached-out eyes that yearn for natural light. The intellect's turned tyrant on us all and made our daily lives into neatly laid-out, over-intellectualized, over-technological exercises in sinister lunacy. Our brains are fed exactitudes, exhausted idioms and petrified notions that leave our bodies dried out and hollow as locust shells. We are severed from ourselves and alien to our sensibilities—fragmented, dissected, pigeon-holed and smothering.[2]

In reaction to this "out of touch" feeling, there is a search today for openness. It has been and still is my own search, too, so I know something of the struggle involved. I discovered that to be more open is to be more in touch with the deep, deep, inner beauty that is in all of us as well.

I am speaking of an openness of the inner person, a relaxation of those defenses that we so often use to protect us from life as it really is—good and bad.

Awareness is another word that expresses this dimension of the new man. I believe I have become more aware of my environment, from the pollution of the air I breathe to the amazing beauty of a single flower bud. I hope I have been learning to be more aware of what is happening to people around me as well. I have also gone through painful times when that awareness has decreased or been blunted or led to agonizing self-appraisal. Openness has meant painful growth for me. On the whole, I believe I am more open to the information coming to me through all my senses, less afraid to interpret it, and more able to trust it, for openness also puts us in touch with our strength.

When openness is overdone, it can be dangerous. The open person must also be disciplined and willing to reject some influences or he leaves himself open to easy manipulation. A healthy, balanced openness is what the new man affirms:

I want to be free to experiment, to sample what life really has to offer. I want to be aware of the magic, the beauty, the pain around me. I've protected myself too long from reality and now I want to be open to live, risk, fail, learn, and celebrate.

I have found an amazing readiness in people today to re-examine old attitudes, rethink outworn doctrines, and to try new styles of relating. I have some friends in their seventies who wrote at Christmas saying that they had taken their first airplane trip just this year. "It was marvelous," they added. I know many people have changed their views on the Vietnam War in recent months as the futility and inhumanity of that conflict has continued. They have had to be open to reconsider their position as new data has arrived. Likewise, I sense a new attitude in many people I know concerning racial prejudice and the need to help change that ugly scene. There is growing concern that our nation open a new relationship with Communist China.

In my work with encounter groups, I often use communication exercises which put people physically in touch with each other. While many confess that this is an experience which is not common to them, they are surprised at themselves that they could enter into it so easily and learn from it so readily. They are surprised at their own openness to express their fear and resistance as well as their openness to grow in their ability to touch appropriately.

In the past year, I have discovered openness in myself as well as others. For years I protested that I couldn't draw a straight line. Now I am joyously studying oil painting for the first time. I have had my first ski lesson and have begun ice skating. While these are not earthshaking changes, they are perhaps symptomatic of a new openness I find in myself.

The field of sensory awareness has helped to give concrete and physical reality to the idea of openness. In a sensory awareness workshop I attended, the instructor asked us to close our eyes and become aware of the feeling of the floor under our bare feet. As we concentrated attention on our feet, I noticed many sensations I had shielded from consciousness. I realized that the floor has texture, and the texture may feel friendly or unfriendly, hard or soft, pleasant or unpleasant. I became aware of the feeling of support that the floor supplies. As I walked, I discovered that I was either accepting the support of the floor by walking relaxedly or rejecting that support by tensing my feet and leg muscles. I felt a deeply religious dimension in the support which is always available through the interface of feet upon ground, and my new openness to accept that support has religious overtones as well.

From many directions there is a new emphasis on breathing and its relationship to awareness. Sensory awareness stresses proper breathing; it is basic to the teaching of yoga; and some branches of psychiatry like Alexander Lowen's bio-energetic analysis now emphasize its importance.

By attending sensory awareness sessions and studying yoga, I have discovered how I have been breathing improperly most of my life, and have been living at less than my potential best. The experience of breathing more deeply has had profound effects in my life, and has helped me develop some discipline in meditation as well. Recently, through bio-energetic analysis, I have been learning how my feelings of anger and sadness and fear have been locked into my muscles, preventing full rhythmic breathing and limiting my full openness as a result. There are always deeper levels of truth about ourselves to be discovered, it seems, if we are willing to endure the pain of the discovery.

When we breathe shallowly, using only a fraction of our lung power as so many people do, we are not living at our full potential. Breathing deeply puts us in touch with our real feelings, helps us feel the messages coming from all the senses, and gives us a sensation of being more alive. When we lock our feelings into our chest, back, and stomach muscles as I have, we restrict our breathing and limit our openness to all reality. Many people fear to get in touch with their real feelings, and so they avoid breathing deeply or feeling deeply. The result is they are not in touch with their inner resources of strength and creativity either. They are not fully alive, open to all that life has to offer. They avoid the pain and miss the joy.

One symbol of the search for openness is the expression "turned-on." There are similarities to being turned-on and the openness I have experienced through yoga and sensory awareness. In her fascinating book, *Turning On,* Rasa Gustaitis has defined what it means to be "turned-on":

To be turned-on is to be with it, into it, right there; to be fully present at whatever one is in at a particular moment, whatever it might bring. It is not a matter of performing well but of fully being; not a question of developing a mature attitude toward adult responsibilities but of experiencing anger, love, grief and joy, perceiving subtle inner and outer events and relationships and responding to them clearly and directly.[3]

Many persons in our culture have had a taste of the "turned-on" experience through drugs, and have later sought more natural and disciplined ways of expanding their awareness. The drug route has dangers, but it has opened personal horizons for many people.

Notes to 4) Open Man

1   Marshall McLuhan, Interview, *Playboy,* March 1969, p. 158.
2   *Look,* January 13, 1970.
3   Rasa Gustaitis, *Turning On* (New York: Signet Books, 1970).

The Good Life, so devoutly sought, has grown blind, bland, banal and numb. Its porcelain, passionless tedium has turned living souls into solid-state circuitry and robbed the body of its feeling. We lie trapped within vast cathedrals of thought, simmering, *hungering for physical contact* yet spinning out our mental energies in empty arabesques. It's time to go, to run, to rise up, fling open the window, thaw the blood, prance high in the wet grass—to shout and feel and seek new rootholds in the nourishing earth.[1]

William Hedgepeth

Whether we can admit it or not, many of us are painfully inhibited about touching and being touched by other people—even those we love. Often, we fail to realize how this separates us from any real emotional contact with those who share our lives.

Reasons are not hard to find. The average American tends to think of bodily contact in terms of sex or combat—both of which are prickly with cultural and psychological taboos. Our Puritan heritage leads many of us to disapprove of any touching as "sensual." And from our frontier days, when pioneers sought the wide-open spaces, and homesteads were miles apart, we often retain an aversion to physical closeness.

Those who've created this invisible barrier have lost something important: the part touch plays in giving encouragement, expressing tenderness, showing emotional support. Touch is a crucial aspect of all human relationships.[2]

Norman M. Lobsenz

Tactile
Man

5

If Marshall McLuhan is right, the twentieth-century electric media—radio, films, telephone, computer, television—have changed the way in which our senses perceive truth and reality. In his words, these new media, in contrast to print, have "enhanced and externalized our entire central nervous systems, thus transforming all aspects of our social and psychic existence."[3]

McLuhan is convinced that the advent of printing diminished the role of the senses of hearing and touch and taste and smell, resulting in a more fragmented man. To my surprise and that of many others, McLuhan speaks of television as heightening the sense of touch.

Unlike film or photograph, television is primarily an extension of the sense of touch rather than of sight, and it is the tactile sense that demands the greatest interplay of all the senses. The secret of TV's tactile power is that the video image is one of low intensity or definition and thus, unlike either photograph or film, offers no detailed information about specific objects but instead involves the active participation of the viewer.[4]

Whether McLuhan's speculation turns out to be correct or not, I have observed that there is a return in our culture to the tactile sense, and I have seen this having wide impact. All over the country, people are being exposed to experiences in which they touch each other. At a recent workshop I led, I invited the group to participate in one of these experiences.

First, I asked the group to close their eyes and become aware of their physical presence in the room. Interspersed with silence, my instructions were something like this:

Now focus your attention on your hands. Wiggle your fingers a little and become aware of the feelings in your hands. Move your hands back and forth so you feel the air between the fingers. Touch one hand with the other. How does it feel to you? What does it say about you? Recall that these hands have done many creative things—writing, sewing, cooking, comforting another, caring. They may have done some things we are sorry about, too. But your hands have potential for great good. They can express and receive many feelings.

After helping the individuals to become aware of their own hands, the group is then asked to make contact with a partner who has been standing face to face with them.

Now slowly move your hands toward the partner in front of you. When you have made contact, explore what those hands are like. Are they rough or smooth? Big or little? Friendly or unfriendly? Relaxed or scared? Be aware of your feelings as you get acquainted with your partner through his hands.

The partners are then asked to explore the space they can reach together—above them, around them, behind them. They are urged to test each other's strength by pushing and carrying on a mock "fight," to make up and then be playful, and finally say goodbye with the hands. At the conclusion of this interaction, the two partners sit down and discuss their feelings about the experience. They often report some initial feelings of awkwardness, which tended to vanish as they relaxed into the experience. Most people report appreciation that they could "meet" another person in this refreshing and revealing way, for they confess that one learns and communicates a great deal with the hands when they are aware of them. I have heard a professor confess that he had known his partner for years but really got to know him for the first time through their encounter with the hands.

I have reported this experience at length to indicate one of the ways in which people are learning to "listen" with their tactile sense. Exercises like this one are suddenly being used very widely. Our youth today seem to have this tactile dimension more naturally, which may explain the popularity of the motorcycle and the sports car, both of which are more in "touch" with the physical reality of the road and offer a tactile satisfaction of their own. While it is more natural to the young, who have had more intensive exposure to television, their parents are also fascinated by experiences which put them back in touch with their senses. And so we read about sense-awakening experiences in which people are picked up by a group and rocked like a baby or learn how to be more free in giving and receiving affection.

In some cultures, people touch a great deal more than in others. We can understand the importance of helping people to touch appropriately when we remember that touching can communicate warmth, caring, support, love, friendship —all things we need desperately in this world today. Touching can be the vehicle of healing as well. The doctor or minister or friend who has eliminated touching from his personal repertoire has limited himself indeed.

So the new man is learning how to touch again, to restore himself to wholeness through contact with other human beings, and with his whole environment. Another sensory experience which is very common today is the trust walk. One partner is led around with his eyes closed while his teammate introduces him to a variety of physical sensations, touching fabrics, feeling cool panes of glass, walking into dark spaces or up flights of stairs. There is a widespread fascination in experiencing familiar objects with the sense of touch. I have heard housewives say they now see things in their own home in a different way because they have touched them and experienced them more deeply.

One sensitive young woman who was attending a workshop where the group was exposed to yoga and sensory awareness training wrote the following words after hearing a presentation on the new man emerging:

The new man tries to be in touch with himself. He sees where he is and he goes in search of meaning—and in search of beauty. All things have their own significance in his becoming. He breathes deeply into himself and it is the breath of life. His body begins to cry out, "Hey, look at me! I'm beautiful and I have good feelings!" He becomes aware of the cold of his isolation and he yearns for warmth. He takes a really deep breath, and reaches toward it, tentatively, and he is received. And it is good. He is lifted up. All around him takes on new dimension. Colors become so vivid they are nearly painful to behold. He begins to notice how many smells and textures are all around, around. He finds himself seeing into the soul of another and sensing need. He does not force or cajole; he gently leads into paths of beauty. He waits. He loves. He leads. He laughs. He waits. He sees. He hears. He knows. He hurts. He cares. He is loved. He is beautiful.[5]

Notes to 5) Tactile Man

1   William Hedgepeth, "A Vision of the Human Revolution,"
    Look, January 13, 1970, p. 60 (italics added).
2   Norman M. Lobsenz, "The Loving Message in a Touch,"
    Woman's Day, February 1970, p. 31.
3   Marshall McLuhan, Interview, *Playboy*, March 1969, p.
    60.
4   Ibid., p. 61.
5   Peggy Rouse.

The silence is broken. After centuries of loneliness and fear we are starting to listen to one another. Perhaps in our homes we are being pushed into listening by our young people because many of them are experimenting with dandies from the medicine cabinets powerful enough to transform them into strangers overnight. Perhaps in our cities we are being pushed into listening because of minorities that may set the streets afire in order to be heard. Perhaps internationally we are being pushed into listening because nations are playing with toys that can blow the whole world to bits if we don't listen to one another. Listening is no longer a luxury, it's a necessity. We may have been scared into communicating, but I, for one, am nevertheless delighted that it is finally happening.

All of us, old and young, black and white and yellow and red, saint and sinner, are individual persons trying to be heard.[1]

Walter Starcke

6

Dialogical Man

Two men were walking along in downtown Detroit one summer afternoon when they noticed an old man with a gray beard shouting at all who passed him. "Nobody will listen to me! I have something important to say and nobody will listen! Nobody will listen to me!"

The two approached him and asked the man, "What is it you want to say?" "Nobody will listen. They're all deaf," he continued loudly. "Nobody will listen to me!" The two tried again. "We'll listen to you. What is it you want to tell us?"

Ignoring them, the old man continued shouting, his arm raised in defiance, "Nobody will listen to me! Nobody cares!"

There is a great hunger for dialogue in the world today, but we have become so accustomed to being turned off and ignored that we are often unprepared when someone is willing to really listen. In the instance of the old man in Detroit, his experience of being ignored had petrified into an illness. He had given up at some point, and his prophecy became self-fulfilling. People had stopped listening.

The hopeful thing is that we are beginning to learn how to listen to each other. Genuine dialogue, which includes both speaking and listening, is beginning to appear and we can find it if we look hard enough. It is a deeply frustrating experience to speak and feel that no one is listening. It was this frustration that led me into my life calling.

As a young pastor serving a church in Seattle, Washington, I felt encouraged by many aspects of my work and the response of the people. I liked them and most of them seemed to like me. We got along well and together we had some high hopes for the future of the congregation. In spite of this, I had some uneasy feelings. I became increasingly aware that preaching was having very little impact on the lives of the people, not just in my church, but in most churches. This uneasiness finally led me to graduate work at Boston University where I could study communication research and relate those insights to the problem of communication in the churches.

The primary discovery I made changed the whole course of my career. I realized increasingly that communication is incomplete when it consists of a monologue, or what the researchers call one-way communication. To achieve full communication, a two-way flow of information is almost required. The communicator needs to listen as well as speak. He needs to hear from the other person whether the message has been heard, understood, accepted, and adopted. This feedback allows him to restate his message in language which can be heard and understood, helps him to try again, modify his goal, and hopefully reach an understanding or common ground with the listener. In other words, *dialogue* is necessary to achieve full communication, but most of us rely heavily on monologues. We don't have time to stop and listen and rephrase and listen some more. We also fear to listen because we might not like what we hear.

If dialogue is so crucial, then it is no wonder that preaching accomplishes so little. The new man is weary of being preached at. He has tasted dialogue and he knows that he has a right to speak as well as to be spoken to. He might put it something like this:

I am no longer willing to sit passively and listen to a monologue with no chance to respond, to question, to disagree, to challenge or correct. I have experienced dialogue here and there, and I now know that I have a right to be heard and I honor myself enough to believe that I have some ideas worth sharing.

The growing insistence on dialogue was expressed in this *New York Times* headline which caught my eye: "Columbia Aids 7 Poverty Projects but Harlem Group Insists on Community Decisions."[2] The story reports a meeting of the Federation of Harlem Organizations, representing 200 groups, to publicly protest the way in which Columbia University was proceeding with seven anti-poverty projects. A prominent complaint was that the university had appointed a director for the program to spend a $10 million Ford Foundation grant without consulting community leaders in Harlem. This growing insistence on being consulted, involved in the dialogue, on matters which affect them, is an expression of the new man.

The new man is more free to speak up, to protest, to insist on his rights, to claim his share in the dialogue. The Columbia University projects were good in themselves, and the Harlem leaders were not protesting the use of anti-poverty money in their neighborhoods. They were simply protesting the one-sided way in which decisions were being made about how the money should be spent.

The new man's insistence on dialogue may also be finding expression in the widespread decline in American church attendance. The traditional Protestant service is centered on the sermon, a twenty- to forty-minute monologue in which there is rarely any opportunity for the parishioner to talk back. It is my own experience that I quickly feel bored as thoughts and reactions come to me which I cannot express. Rarely are discussion opportunities provided so I can raise with exciting new approaches to worship, stressing the release of spontaneity and creativity in the people. He was free and yet responsible and creative, rooted in the tradition out of which he had come. Henk was an exciting person to be around.

The new man is first of all a free man. Not totally free, of course. No man is ever totally free. But there is a new freedom breaking forth in the world today. I see it in the freedom to speak out in one's own behalf and in behalf of others. I see it in the freedom to protest wrong and insist on change, and in man's freedom to break out of stifling molds that inhibit his life and creativity.

I see the new freedom in a Rosa Parks standing up for her rights on a bus in Montgomery, Alabama, and refusing to be pushed around by arrogant Whites who would treat her as less than human. I see the new free man in those two hundred parishioners who walked out of the cathedral in the middle of their bishop's sermon defending the Pope's edict on birth control. The new man is more free than his forebears, less fearful, less inclined to be used. If the new man could speak to us, he might put it like this:

I insist on being free. Free to be alive, to be honest, to be myself, not just to be what somebody else expects me to be. I have my own destiny to fulfill, my own unique gifts to develop, my own thing to do. I do not accept the rigid, legalistic systems of the past. I want to be free of that so I can find a new morality that makes more sense for today, one that puts people before rules. I want to be turned-on, fully alive, fully aware of the joy and excitement that life has to offer.

The new man's insistence on freedom may be seen in the great social movements of history, but it may also be sensed in more subtle everyday ways as well. The new man is more free in his dress, his thought, his language, and his actions.

The new man's new freedom in language is illustrated by

my questions, make my contribution. So, like many others I know, I look for opportunities where I can speak as well as listen. I'm not interested in being bored anymore.

There are signs of hope and change, too. Some churches are beginning to recognize the importance of providing small groups, discussion opportunities, and creative new forms of worship. Some social agencies are beginning to listen to the people as they make their decisions. Educational designs are beginning to reflect awareness of the need for dialogue as well as lectures.

About a year ago I received a tempting invitation to speak at a summer conference at Lake Louise in the Canadian Rockies. I love the Pacific Northwest and the rugged mountains there. I would have delighted in an opportunity to take my family west with a large portion of the expense paid. But in good conscience I could not accept. The program called for one speaker after another, with ten-minute breaks between speeches.

This was once considered good education, to assemble a lineup of headliners to pour information and inspiration into the empty buckets of the listeners. But we now know that people are not empty buckets, and we must modify our educational styles to fit this reality. People may once have acted like they were empty buckets, but they won't sit still much longer for such treatment. When I accept speaking invitations now, I usually request opportunity for dialogue with the audience in some form. I find this much more satisfying and so do my listeners. I also have found that when I ask for such an opportunity, the program planners are usually pleased to include it. They are open to innovation but sometimes need a little reminder or a little push to make it happen.

We are not always happy when we encounter the dialogical man putting pressure on us to let him into the decision-making process. We are not always happy about those who want community control of public schools or who want representation for their minority on the police force and the city council. But on the whole, these are expressions of strength for which we should rejoice.

The new man is dialogical man. He wants in on the act, and knows he has a right to be in on it. It may be uncomfortable to change all our social structures which have relied on a more authoritarian, one-way approach to communication, but we will emerge with a much sounder and healthier social situation.

Notes to 6) Dialogical Man

1   Walter Starcke, *The Ultimate Revolution* (New York: Harper & Row, 1969), p. 9.
2   *New York Times,* May 12, 1968, p. 68.

People are also troubled because of the new participative mood that exists today. It's a do-it-yourself
society; every layman wants to get into the act.
Emerson's "do your own thing" has become the
cliché of the times. People no longer accept being
passive members. They now want to be active
changers.[1]

Richard E. Farson

All the individual revolutions we are witnessing on
the campuses, in the streets, in the laboratories, in
every conceivable area of life, add up to one thing.
Man is now refusing to live any longer by laws that
dehumanize him. MAN IS COMING OF AGE. Man
is finding out who he is, and he's wonderful to behold. He sees no reason to continue putting up with
sickness. He's going to rebel and rebel until the
cause of revolution is eliminated.[2]

Walter Starcke

Participative Man

7

The new man is not only responsible and dialogical, but participative as well. While participative man is a first cousin to responsible man and dialogical man, there is an important difference. It is possible to be responsible in the way we conduct our personal affairs without entering the public arena. By making a decision *not* to do something, we may be exercising our role as responsible man. Dialogical man, likewise, may satisfy his hunger for dialogue through speaking and listening. The participative streak in the new man extends the responsible and dialogical dimensions to the level of action for others as well as self.

If the new man could speak for himself, he might say:

> I am concerned about the kind of world I live in, and I feel responsible to improve that world. Not only that, but I insist on having a voice in shaping those laws and institutions that govern my world. I am willing to speak up against unjust conditions, but furthermore, I am willing to put my body where my words are and risk something to effect necessary change.

Increasingly, we are finding participative man insisting on his right to influence his world. We can see this new-man-ness in the civil rights movement, in many of the campus revolts, in the peace marches, the women's rebellion, and many of the other protest movements blossoming today. It would be much more comforting to many of our leaders today if we could condemn all those who are "troublemakers" and cross them off our list of decent human beings. Alas, to dismiss the protest leaders so glibly is not only irresponsible but stupid. Many of the protests are the last ditch effort of responsible persons who have exhausted every other means to achieve valid goals. A depth analysis of a situation like the Columbia University student occupation in 1968 reveals that there were deep provocations by the university that led to the takeover of five buildings by students. The brutality of the police raids to drive the students out mobilized the faculty to express their strong solidarity with the student cause.

According to the *New York Times*, large numbers of the university faculty, who had primarily confined their concern to the classroom, became involved in lobbying, handing out pamphlets, and joining countless committees in support of the student cause. While it is certainly true that some students engaged in irresponsible acts such as destroying valuable books and damaging property, the basic thrust of the student takeover was to call dramatic public attention to some of the irresponsible practices of the university.[3]

One faculty member, chairman of the anthropology department, was quoted in the *Times* as admitting, "I began to listen to the students and realized that they had cause, and had been calling out to us for two or three years before they were driven to the occupation of the buildings by an insensitive administration." He admitted further that the faculty had been buried in its work, ignoring student problems.

This is the basic cause of the antiquated structure we have at Columbia, and I feel part of the guilt myself. Things have to be reversed. It's almost as if the faculty and students have been here at the pleasure of the administration. It's going to have to be that the administration is here at the pleasure of the faculty and students.[4]

Another faculty member, a professor of English, put it in plain terms:

What happened to most of us during the past week is that we learned, through student willingness to stick their necks out, how profound the dissatisfaction is. I've long been aware that the administration is much too greatly separated from the students. If I and other faculty members haven't done more, it's because we have been preoccupied with courses. This led, in part, to the regrettable acceptance of the status quo.[5]

A young history professor added this note, "These students aren't creating a revolution and they know it. They are creating conditions in which a whole lot of overdue reforms are going to occur. Columbia is going to be a fantastic place."[6] Not all faculty members agreed with the quoted parties, of course.

We should rightly be impatient with those persons who, for political reasons or out of ignorance, condemn all protests as immoral and illegal. The thoughtful citizen should express himself only after he has carefully studied the facts in the *particular* situation, listened to both sides, and evaluated the necessity of the protest action.

The appearance of participative man has hardly left any strata of our culture untouched. A newspaper headline recently announced: "Priests for Loyalty, not Obedience." The article cited some of the proceedings at a meeting of American priests in New Orleans, including the group's insistence on a priest's right to due process of law when punished by his bishop. One priest was quoted as saying, "There is great loyalty to bishops among our priests today, but without subservience. They want a share in the decision-making processes of the church—not simply to take orders from above."[7]

People simply do not want to be treated as objects anymore. They will not be folded, spindled, and mutilated by uncaring institutions— or not much longer. This was demonstrated in a small Swiss town, Chur, in 1969, when 70 priests gathered in front of the palace where Roman Catholic prelates were meeting. The 112 cardinals, archbishops, and bishops had convened from 18 nations to discuss the crisis in their priesthood. They not only discussed the crisis; they had to deal with one on their doorstep.

The leader of the priests' group, a fiery Frenchman with a bullhorn, announced that the servants of Jesus Christ "were now joining the world's students and workers to demand better human conditions."[8] The priests were calling for three basic reforms. They wanted the right to be more active in political and social affairs, the right to marry, and the democratic election of their leaders. While the assembled dignitaries did not permit the protestors to enter, they did pass a resolution acknowledging that priests today want an "authentic co-responsibility" within the Roman Church.[9]

The emergence of participative man is widespread, and is by no means confined to protest or negative actions. There are many constructive steps being taken to grant the participation even before it becomes a necessity. The move at Fordham University to turn over majority control on the board of trustees to laymen after 122 years of Jesuit control is an example of this peaceful movement toward a more participative society. Such a change is difficult to imagine, although there had been considerable student and faculty pressure for reforms.

The stories of men like Ralph Nader and John Banzhaf are interesting in the light of participative man. Banzhaf, a twenty-nine-year-old lawyer, organized a group called ASH (Action on Smoking and Health). Banzhaf demanded free time from the nation's television stations for antismoking messages and, surprisingly, was granted that right. Last fall, he taught a course at George Washington University Law School on unfair trade practices. The sixty students got fired up by the course and immediately organized activist groups to investigate poverty abuses, unfair television advertising, gasoline frauds, and other injustices.[10]

There is a new spirit abroad, and participative man is on the loose.

Notes to 7) Participative Man

1   Richard E. Farson, "How Could Anything That Feels So Bad Be So Good?" *Saturday Review,* September 6, 1969, p. 20.
2   Walter Starcke, *The Ultimate Revolution* (New York: Harper & Row, 1969), p. 17.
3   *New York Times,* May 12, 1968, p. 69.
4   Ibid. © 1968 by The New York Times Company. Reprinted by permission.
5   Ibid.
6   Ibid.
7   *Detroit News,* March 30, 1969, p. 17A.
8   *Time,* July 18, 1969.
9   Ibid.
10 *Time,* March 2, 1970, pp. 15–16.

Ecumenical Man

The new man does not really believe in religious denominations anymore. Even when he belongs to one religious group, even when his family tradition has been associated with that religious group for years, he does not believe in its preeminence over other groups anymore. How could he? The new man has grown up in a Presbyterian family, attended the Methodist Sunday school, joined an Episcopal senior high fellowship, dated a Baptist girl and a Quaker, ran around with a Christian Scientist pal and a Pentecostal, married a Roman Catholic, plays golf with a Jew, has Greek Orthodox neighbors, and sends his kids to the nearest church which happens to be the United Church of Christ. In the meantime, his sister has married a Methodist, and . . . .

The new man might phrase it this way if he could speak for himself:

I do not any longer believe in the superiority of my religious group over any other. I am aware that all groups have their contribution to make and that all have their unique blindnesses. I honor my religion and I believe it is right for me, but I can honor the validity of many other groups as well, and I believe in working together in every possible way.

The ecumenical spirit is abroad in many forms, and the news media are filled with examples. A recent headline in the *Detroit News* read as follows: "Eastern Religions Gain Interest: Hindu Joins U-D Faculty." The article begins in an interesting way. "Ten years ago, the only people who taught theology at the University of Detroit were Jesuit priests. But teaching religion today at U. of D. are three Protestant clergymen, a Catholic layman, several Jewish instructors—and now a Hindu." The article goes on to announce the appointment of a new professor from India who will start a program of study in Eastern religions.[1]

Last summer I was invited to share the leadership of a conference for 400 Roman Catholic nuns. The leadership team of four included a Roman priest, a Catholic layman, and two Protestants, assisted by a large group of nuns and priests who served as group leaders. I found it an enlightening and delightful experience as I entered into a world of relationships about which I had known very little. Just a few years ago, such openness and cooperation was unheard of.

I recently had a telephone call from a friend, who is a nun, inviting me to speak to the religion classes at the Roman Catholic elementary school where she teaches. Many of the youngsters had never met a Protestant churchman before, and they asked very intelligent, searching questions. The school was observing Christian unity week. The experience helped all of us to understand each other better, in spite of our clear differences of viewpoint on many issues. The fact that there is enough openness for this kind of interchange to take place is an encouraging sign of ecumenical man's emergence.

Roman Catholic priests may now be found studying in Protestant theological schools and Protestants studying in Roman Catholic schools. Some Roman Catholic schools are merging facilities with Protestant schools in a deeper expression of the unity trend. At the Institute for Advanced Pastoral Studies, Protestant church leaders from over fifty denominations have come to study for ten days at a time, and

Roman Catholic leaders as well. Lay men and women from both groups attend conferences there as well, and Jewish leaders may soon join them. These ecumenical study conferences have been in progress since 1957. The exciting thing to observe is how denominational labels are forgotten as twenty men and women arrive to live together for ten days. They meet each other as persons apart from their religious differences and learn that they can live together and feel deeply for each other as human beings.

I will never forget a conference I once led at the Institute. Twenty-four persons gathered for a week to study small group leadership. A Roman priest and a nun were among those attending. In the course of the week, the group experienced both pain and joy together, and a close sense of community developed. Each evening, the young priest said mass before retiring, and he would invite any who wished to join him. On the final evening of the conference, we concluded our final session together about 10 P.M. The first new snow of the winter season was on the ground. It was cold, crisp, and clear, with a brilliant full moon adding its magic to the snow. Silently, one by one, we went out into the snow to walk and ponder the meaning of the week for us. We reassembled silently in a large parlor, sitting on the carpet while Chuck said mass for us all, inviting us to share our thoughts and reflections. It was a deeply moving occasion, made possible in part by the ecumenical spirit abroad in the world today. Chuck probably would not have been granted permission for this ecumenical mass had he consulted his authorities in the church, but he followed his own conscience rather than canon law. The new man is unwilling to follow blind authority when his conscience tells him that authority is wrong.

On occasion, the ecumenical realities are present in the

person of one individual. The dental hygienist who cleans my teeth grew up in a Roman Catholic home, adopted a Protestant faith as a youth, then became a convert to Judaism after falling in love with the young man who became her husband.

For many years now, Protestant groups have been moving together, reversing the trend of earlier American history when schism was the more common pattern. In recent years, the historic merger of the Evangelical Reformed Church and the Congregational Christian Churches created a new denomination, the United Church of Christ. The Evangelical United Brethren Church merged with the Methodists to form the United Methodist Church. Presbyterians have moved back together, and Lutherans have begun to combine forces in impressive ways. These are only a few examples of a major historical trend.

The most impressive merger possibility in the ecumenical world today is the proposal to bring together nine major American denominations. The Consultation on Church Union has presented a unity plan which could bring together the United Methodist Church, the Episcopal Church, the United Presbyterian Church in the U.S.A., the United Church of Christ, the Christian Church (Disciples of Christ), the African Methodist Episcopal Church, the Presbyterian Church in the U.S. (Southern), the African Methodist Episcopal Zion Church, and the Christian Methodist Episcopal Church. That this impressive array of religious groups, with such widely divergent histories and rituals, can seriously consider unity is good news indeed. The proposed name of this group is "The Church of Christ Uniting," to indicate the spirit of openness to others who may later wish to join.

Beyond the narrow confines of Protestantism, there are

signs of hope in the growing cooperation between major religious groups on many projects where their common concern for humanity brings them together. A recent news article from Geneva announced the creation of an Ecumenical Development Fund designed to finance projects for promoting social justice and self-reliance in the poorer nations. The Fund hopes to begin with $10 million donated by the 242 Protestant and Orthodox churches affiliated with the World Council of Churches.[2] The Council-affiliated churches have long worked together in many areas, including the welfare and relief work of Church World Service. Another encouraging sign is the emergence of community interfaith councils replacing or rising parallel to the Christian councils of churches, which have been primarily Protestant. The new interfaith councils tend to include Protestant, Catholic, and Jewish representation.

A recent report adds another hopeful dimension to the ecumenical scene. It is the statement by major press services that Roman Catholic bishops of the United States have taken significant steps toward negotiating officially with the National Council of Churches, the predominantly Protestant and Orthodox body. To quote the Associated Press, "A historic Christian alliance at the national level could be the result." While this may be undue optimism, the fact is that there are steps toward greater unity being taken every day in many places and many ways. We cannot but feel hopeful about these efforts to bridge centuries-old rifts between human groups.

The big question which only time will answer is this: Will the religious groups move toward unity and renewal fast enough to serve and reach the new man who is losing interest? The new man emerging is tired of the antiquated and often boring experience he finds in most churches and synagogues, regardless of the hoary traditions represented by those experiences. They simply do not speak to him anymore. If the forms are too rigid and the people who determine them are too rigid to change rapidly enough, there may not be any people left in the churches to change for. Ecumenicity may arrive too late to reach the new man.

Notes to 8) Ecumenical Man

1 *Detroit News,* February 7, 1970.
2 *New York Times,* February 22, 1970.

Now the old concepts of territoriality, of property ownership, of nationalism and patriotism—of race and color and creed—that once were the ingredients for survival of this species on this planet, become turned inside out. The global man, the human man, may become the cell of the new society in which the use of the territorial imperative will become an exercise as meaningless as the Crusades. We have long since given up war as a means of spreading religious ideas; we now move into an era in which we may have to give up war as a means of spreading political and economic ideas. And this will take a new kind of man, and a new kind of family unit. Hopefully—for the time grows short—both already are emerging.[1]

Don Fabun

The world of human thought today presents a very remarkable spectacle, if we choose to take note of it. Joined in an inexplicable unifying movement men who are utterly opposed in education and in faith find themselves brought together, intermingled, in their common passion for a double truth; namely, that there exists a physical Unity of beings, and that they themselves are living and active parts of it. It is as though a new and formidable mountain chain had arisen in the landscape of the soul, causing ancient categories to be reshuffled and uniting higgledy-piggledy on every slope the friends and enemies of yesterday.[2]

Pierre Teilhard de Chardin

9

World
Man

World Man. Global Man. Universal Man. By whatever name, there is a new spirit emerging in man which is impatient with narrow nationalisms and which is increasingly aware of the oneness that binds all men together. To be sure, there are still conflicts that continue to pit nations against each other in horribly destructive ways. To be sure, there are still hatreds smoldering between peoples which separate them and will continue to separate them for a long time. We should not pretend these realities are not there or expect that they will go away very soon. But we must also keep in sight the hopeful realities, the signs of growing global unity that are just as real as the Vietnam War and the conflict in the Middle East.

One of the hopeful realities is the fact that in the spring of 1970, there was a meeting in San Francisco to celebrate the twenty-fifth anniversary of the founding of the United Nations. While some of the dreams and hopes have not become actualities, some fantastic accomplishments have been recorded by the United Nations, and the peoples of the world are moving closer together. There is a World Health Organization, a Food and Agriculture Organization, an International Labor Office, and an International Bank. UNICEF exists. The United Nations Development Fund operates. Many, many other international organizations function to bring us closer to a harmony of world life that could eventually result in a warless world community.

In addition to the movements already mentioned, there is growing world concern over control of the environment. When we discover industrial fallout from Britain's factories in Sweden and Russia, and lead deposits from gasoline in the ice at the North Pole, we cannot ignore the need for international cooperation to save us from destroying our own life space.

If given a voice, the new man might express his feelings this way:

I cannot any longer buy the myth that says my country is wiser and stronger and somehow superior to all others. I know that I am a citizen of the world first, sharing in common many concerns with people of all nations. My country has virtues and makes mistakes—like all the others. I want a world where my children can grow up in peace and brother-hood with all kinds of men.

After all, the new man has grown up in a French-Canadian home, gone to school with Whites, Negroes, Puerto Ricans, Jews, Jamaicans, Irishmen, and Poles. He has been stationed in Morocco and Germany, visited all of Europe, married a Japanese war bride, adopted two Korean orphans, has a Lithuanian sister-in-law, and drives an Italian car. He eats pizza, shrimp chow mein, and Russian rye bread, and wears an African sport shirt. His personal history is a world-oriented history in almost every aspect of his life. To deny the unity of his world, he must now deny himself.

The radio age has helped man become aware of his wider world, the transoceanic telephone has added a dimension of instant two-way communication, and instantaneous television via satellite has brought us even closer. When people can stand in the streets of Paris and watch American astronauts land on the moon, something ineradicable has taken place. The astronauts represented man, not the United States.

Marshall McLuhan has spoken about this growing relationship of men with each other as a result of the impact of television:

The implosion of electric technology is transmogrifying literate, fragmented man into a complex and depth-structured human being with a deep emotional awareness of his complete interdependence with all of humanity.[3]

In addition to the continual erosion of narrow nationalism by mass communication (including old cowboy movies), the increasing ease of transportation brings people together into a world culture. Last Sunday I took my three youngsters to a movie and stage show. While we were waiting for Bozo the Clown to appear, I found myself in conversation with the mother seated beside me. She had fled Hungary in 1956 at the time of the unsuccessful rebellion, and had eventually landed in the United States and married a surgeon here. She mentioned that her mother still lives in Hungary. I immediately had images of this poor woman separated from her mother for life by harsh political realities, and a feeling of sadness crept over me—until she explained that her mother flies to this country once a year to visit the family! I hardly see my own mother more than once a year and she lives only 800 miles away. The world is rapidly becoming smaller, and we are rapidly discovering that we are brothers with men everywhere.

Kenneth Boulding has spoken in more depth of the impact of world transportation:

Furthermore the rapid and easy transportation which post-civilization permits makes it much more difficult to maintain culture traits in isolation. Civilizations could flourish at the same time on the earth which had little or no contact one with another. The Mayan civilization certainly had no contact with Rome, and Rome had very little contact with China. . . . Now, however, it is as easy to go halfway around the world as it used to be to go to a neighboring town, and under these circumstances an enormous process of cultural mixture is taking place which can hardly help producing much greater uniformity even in a few hundred years. It is doubtful whether a single world language will emerge in the near future, but certainly in styles of clothing, housing, mass entertainment, and transportation it is becoming increasingly hard to distinguish one part of the world from another.[4]

Huston Smith, the philosopher, speaks of a new world culture emerging in which the strengths of Chinese, Indian, and Western traditions are blended. The social stability of the Chinese culture, the spiritual discipline of India, and the concept of individual liberty seem to be feeding into the creation of a great new world civilization, according to Smith.[5]

Teilhard de Chardin, the great French scientist and thinker, whose thought has provided much support and inspiration for this volume, speaks of a collective human consciousness which increases with each generation, drawing men together until ultimately there will be a unity of human consciousness. Teilhard's thought is difficult and complicated to follow (for me at least), but there is great lucidity in his optimism about the evolution of the human spirit. There is a "profound unity of the world within and around us," he says.[6]

There is in the world today a rising spread of compassion, a rising horror of all kinds of war and cruelty and deprivation, a growing ability to "feel with" those of other cultures and backgrounds, a growing unity that draws all mankind into its warm fold. A new man is emerging, and he is aware of his citizenship as a world man.

Notes to 9) World Man

1 Don Fabun, *The Dynamics of Change* (Englewood Cliffs, N. J.: Prentice-Hall, 1967), pp. 26–27.
2 Pierre Teilhard de Chardin, *The Future of Man*, tr. Norman Denny (New York: Harper & Row, 1964), p. 32.
3 Marshall McLuhan, Interview, *Playboy*, March 1969, p. 70.
4 Kenneth Boulding, *The Meaning of the Twentieth Century* (New York: Harper & Row, 1964), p. 18.
5 Paraphrased from an excellent summary in Rasa Gustaitis, *Turning On* (New York: Signet Books, 1970), p. xii.
6 Teilhard de Chardin, op. cit., p. 32.

Will we then find life to be only a stage, though an essential one, in a cosmic evolution of which our evolving awareness is beginning to become aware? Will we discover that only *without* spaceships can we reach the galaxies; that only *without* cyclotrons can we know the interior of atoms? To venture beyond the fantastic accomplishments of this physically fantastic age, sensory perception must combine with the extrasensory, and I suspect that the two will prove to be different faces of each other. I believe it is through sensing and thinking about such concepts that great adventures of the future will be found.[1]

Charles Lindbergh

It asks of us, for example, a new dimension of faith, a deeper prayer; yes, and that we even be another kind of person. We are surrounded by extraordinary possibilities and extraordinary graces for us, for the Church, for all mankind. We are, as it were, in ascension, moving towards new heights. No longer within a particular small culture, a provincial culture, perhaps a ghetto culture, we have become citizens not only of a country but of the world; citizens, indeed, of the cosmos.[2]

Father Edward Farrell

Cosmic Man

Like so many people, I have a friend with psychic gifts. Charles didn't cultivate these powers, but unusual things have happened to him on occasion. I remember the time I stopped to visit Charles and heard a very strange story. He had been taking a short nap before supper. He was lying on his bed half-awake when he had the sensation that he was floating in the air above his body. He found himself leaving the room while his body remained on the bed. He soon realized that he was listening to a conversation between two married friends of his. They were arguing bitterly, and Charles felt rather embarrassed to be listening to such a personal exchange. He soon found himself back on his bed.

Before going to supper, Charles wrote down exactly what he could remember of the conversation, sealed it in an envelope and wrote the time on the outside. After his meal, Charles put on his coat and went to see the two friends upon whom he had accidentally eavesdropped shortly before. Upon arriving, he handed them the envelope and asked them to read it. As they read, their faces became redder and redder, and they confessed that the words were exactly what they had been saying only a few hours before.

I personally do not doubt Charles' story. Increasingly, there seems to be evidence that the spirit of man is not tied to his physical body, and the weight of the data is extremely difficult to dismiss, even if we prefer not to believe a particular story. I recently found a paperback book in the local drugstore filled with stories of persons who have had the experience of leaving the body. We seem to be entering a period of more openness to the possibilities of extrasensory perception, psychic phenomena, and the existence of life beyond.

One of my earliest experiences with Eastern meditation was so dramatic that I shall never forget it. At the conclusion of a yoga lesson, our teacher invited us to enter a period of relaxed meditation, either lying on our backs on the floor or sitting in the Buddhist position. I chose to try sitting meditation for the first time. Using one of the simple methods for concentration suggested by the teacher, I soon found myself in the midst of an experience of incredible beauty and awesomeness. For a while I saw a flowing variety of magnificent colors, constantly changing but breathtaking in color and form, psychedelic in effect.

I want to emphasize that this experience of color and beauty was not the product of my conscious imagination. I was an amazed observer, not the producer of the images, and they seemed much more real and vivid than any dream or fantasy I can recall. I felt I was in touch with a dimension of reality I had never touched before, but which filled me with joy and peace. Perhaps the most memorable part of the experience was near the end when I felt I was floating or flying out through space. I felt I was moving at a great rate of speed, and stars or bright lights would become brighter as I approached them. As I came close to one of these warm, friendly lights (this was the feeling tone I associated with them), they would suddenly burst into huge, magnificent bouquets of blue cornflowers or petunias and pass on by. I saw them in vivid detail and felt their fantastic perfection and beauty. I somehow knew that these lights and flowers were related to God and were manifestations of him. I had no fear at all during this experience, just awe.

I couldn't wait to share the beauty and joy of this moment with friends.

I later associated this meditation experience with what I felt during the movie *2001: A Space Odyssey* as the spaceship hurtled out through space, and we were shown incredible, fast-moving sequences of color and beauty and cosmic membership that I found briefly through meditation. With LSD, one can get there the American way—without self-discipline and pain. But once having been there, once having found the way it is natural that the person should not want to lose touch with that experience of beauty, presuming that he had a "good trip" with his LSD. (There are many barriers to having a good trip, including bad drugs, negative influences in the environment, etc.) The encouraging part to me is the fact that many people are turning to meditation as a more natural way and less dangerous way to find their path back to what they discovered chemically with drugs. There is a feeling of weakness in being dependent upon the drugs to find peace and beauty, and there is the danger of becoming so dependent that one finds permanent escape from the harsh realities of life via the drug route.

The amazing mind of Marshall McLuhan has offered us some insights into this emerging dimension of cosmic man. While his words are often challenging and his thought difficult to grasp, I have always found it rewarding to struggle with the deep meanings he wrestles with. Try this statement of McLuhan for example:

Tribal man is tightly sealed in an integral collective awareness that transcends conventional boundaries of time and space. As such, the new society will be one mythic integration, a resonating world akin to the old tribal echo chamber where magic will live again: a world of ESP. The current interest of youth in astrology, clairvoyance, and the occult is no coincidence. Electric technology, you see, does not require words any more than a digital computer requires numbers. Electricity makes possible—and not in the distant future, either—an amplification of human consciousness on a world scale, without any verbalization at all.[3]

The interviewer speaking with McLuhan when he made the above statement then asked if he was speaking of global telepathy. "Precisely," he replied. And he added this comment:

Via the computer, we could logically proceed from translating languages to bypassing them entirely in favor of an integral cosmic consciousness somewhat similar to the collective unconscious envisioned by Bergson. The computer thus holds out the promise of a technologically engendered state of universal understanding and unity, a state of absorption in the logos that could knit mankind into one family and create a perpetuity of collective harmony and peace. This is the *real* use of the computer, not to expedite marketing or solve technical problems but to speed the process of discovery and orchestrate terrestial—and eventually galactic—environments and energies. Psychic communal integration, made possible at last by the electronic media, could create the universality of consciousness.[4]

I do not pretend to grasp the full import of McLuhan's thought in these words, but they do fill me with hope and a vision of the unity of mankind that transcends the physical limitations we have imposed on ourselves by failing to admit our psychic potential.

I find confirmation of this future possibility in a remarkable statement by Charles Lindbergh, published by *Life* magazine just prior to the historic 1969 moon landing by American astronauts. Lindbergh had been asked to write an article for *Life* on the great adventures in history, but Lindbergh refused. He wrote a long letter to *Life* explaining why he could not write such an article, and the letter was so powerful that they asked him if they could publish it.

In his letter, Lindbergh speaks of his life spent on the frontiers of the human search. When the art of flying began to develop into a science, he lost interest and looked for another frontier. He returned to the contemplation of life, biological research, the question of life and death, and man's mystical qualities. He began studying "supersensory phenomena" and flew to India to study yoga. He spent some time with Robert Goddard in the 1930's at Goddard's experimental rocket-testing station in New Mexico. Out of this life of search and study, Lindbergh now makes some startling predictions about the future of man.

Decades spent in contact with science and its vehicles have directed my mind and senses to areas beyond their reach. I now see scientific accomplishment as a path, not an end; a path leading to the disappearing in mystery. Science, in fact, forms many paths branching from the trunk of human progress; and on every periphery they end in the miraculous. Following these paths far enough, and long enough, one must eventually conclude that science itself is a miracle—like the awareness of man arising from and then disappearing in the apparent nothingness of space. Rather than nullifying religion and proving that "God is dead," science enhances spiritual values by revealing the magnitudes and minitudes—from cosmos to atom—through which man extends and of which he is composed.[5]

When Lindbergh says that we may someday reach the galaxies without spaceships, that we will learn to use sensory perception combined with the extrasensory, we touch the breathtaking world of the new man emerging, a man who will be free to roam the cosmos to which he belongs and of which he is an integral part.

Notes to 10) Cosmic Man

1 Charles Lindbergh, "A Letter from Lindbergh," *Life*, July 4, 1969, p. 61.
2 Fr. Edward Farrell, "Prayer Is a Hunger," *Gothic*, Winter 1968–69.
3 Marshall McLuhan, Interview, *Playboy*, March 1969, p. 72.
4 Ibid.
5 Lindbergh, op. cit., p. 60b.

Many others believe they are participating in a revolution of the spirit. Institutional churches may be dying, but there are religious torrents running among the young and the old, among people of all ages and places.

. . . . .

The material resources of the earth are limited and must be conserved. But limitations on the resources of the spirit—the functioning of the mind, the outreach of human sympathy, the awareness that many men still have of an awesome presence given the name of God—have not yet been discovered.[1]

Frank K. Kelly

There is a big boom in mysticism in this country. Americans are turning to witchcraft, astrology, fortune-telling, satanism, and psychic phenomena and other occult practices in what appears to be a search for spiritual experience. Although some may do it for laughs, books, magazines, periodicals on the subject abound. There are waiting lists at libraries for the more popular volumes; the writings of the late Bishop James Pike gave impetus to an already well-established trend. It's part of the overall quest for mystique, at a time when some feel let down by traditional religions.[2]

J. Oscar Frenette

11

Spiritual
Man

There is a curious paradox in the American religious scene today. Attendance is declining in many churches of the major religious groups and there appears to be a widespread decline in the number of those applying for religious vocations. At the same time, there are many signs of a religious resurgence, a spiritual search that is taking many varied and exotic forms from classes in yoga to a craze for astrology and the occult.

All this encourages me in my conviction that the new man is a deeply spiritual man. Precisely because he is a spiritual man, he does not find meaning any longer in the formalized, fossilized, antiseptic, impersonal worship services in so many churches today. That form is dead or dying, and the new man is usually to be found elsewhere searching for religious vitality.

As I review the occasions in recent years when I have had a deeply moving experience which my intuition told me was related to the living spirit of God, most of these experiences have not been in church. I have found this vitality in a human relations training group, in yoga meditation, standing barefoot in the ocean in the moonlight, in loving and being loved, in the joy of a child, in honest sharing with another person, or in the incredible beauty of a single flower.

I shall never forget one experience at the Esalen Institute in California along the magnificent Big Sur coast. I was attending a five-day workshop on "Unmasking Ourselves" led by a noted research psychiatrist affiliated with the University of California in Berkeley. One of the primary tools our leader used to help us see ourselves, accept ourselves, and to grow as persons was a series of meditation experiences. Here was a sophisticated practitioner, an authority on medical research and gestalt therapy methods using *meditation* as a primary tool for helping people! For the meditation time one day, to my surprise, his instruction to us was, "Let your body do the will of God, and observe what your body does. If the term God is not meaningful for you, imagine there is a God and do what he might want you to do." My experiences in that workshop, and especially in the meditation times, were deeply confirming and strengthening and were to me genuine religious experiences.

Experiences such as this have led me to affirm that "the world is becoming the church." I attach great meaning to this statement; it is not a glib comment. The world is becoming the church. The spirit of God is free in the world (as, of course, it has been all along). In some places, even the churches are becoming the church. But the vital, flowing, living spirit of God is more easily found right now outside the churches, which is a cause for sadness. Some church groups may find strength and freedom enough to tap that spirit, but many others will die of hardened arteries or heart failure in the years ahead.

The *New York Times* News Service recently issued an article entitled, "Young Move Away from Church to New Religion." To quote:

A new religious intensity appears to be making itself felt on American campuses. It rejects the standard faiths, but some scholars and theologians say it has all the elements of a religion to go with the "counter culture" developing among a large segment of the nation's youth.

The characteristics of the movement are not being defined

98

along lines normally understood as religious, but in terms of the younger generation's emphasis on love, celebration and the search for meaning.[3]

The article goes on to cite the heightened interest today among students for the mystical, the symbolic and ultimate questions. They are enrolling in religion courses in record numbers, particularly courses on Eastern religions. One university student spoke for many others when she said, "I'm not going away from religion, just from the church."[4]

There is much speculation about the motivation for this new deepening interest among the young in religion of all sorts. One prime cause may well be their disillusionment with the culture of their parents. They see their mothers and fathers attending churches and synagogues, but in their day to day behavior more concerned with amassing wealth and property than in concern for persons or social justice. The parents seem more anxious about their social standing in the community than in the pain of their own children. The parents are harsh about the use of marijuana among the young, but drink themselves unconscious and destroy their health with tobacco. The contradictions in this materialistic culture may be a strong stimulant for the young to seek a more meaningful existence.

And, of course, the new religious impulse is not limited to the young by any means. Persons of many age levels are seeking as well. I recently visited a group called the Self-Realization Fellowship which meets weekly for a meditation service in downtown Detroit. To my surprise, where I had expected a small group of perhaps fifteen or twenty persons, I found an auditorium filled with several hundred persons of all ages. The service itself was a curious combination of Eastern meditation and elements of a typical Protestant worship service.

The current interest in unusual religious forms may be felt

in the mass media, especially in the magazines on news-stands today.

A 1968 issue of the *Saturday Evening Post* displayed on its cover a huge picture of the Maharishi Mahesh Yogi with the Beatles and movie star Mia Farrow. The accompanying story chronicled the wide following the Maharishi had among the famous from many lands, a following which has now declined. A recent issue of *McCall's* magazine was devoted to "The Occult Explosion," detailing the wide current interest in astrology, tarot cards, seances, and satan worship.

The *New York Times* has helped us understand the genuinely religious dimension of another current expression of the mystical, witchcraft. The article includes an interview with Sybil Leek, a widely known witch who claims there are at least 400 witches' covens in the United States. Miss Leek spoke about witchcraft as a religion:

> We are entering the age of Aquarius, and people are searching. They are searching for a religion where they don't have to live a God-like life, a religion that acknowledges them as human beings. Witchcraft is a return to nature religion. It teaches people their place in the universe and helps them see religion much more clearly—as a real thing and not as a fantasy world.[5]

Miss Leek mentioned the special appeal that witchcraft seems to have for youth: "They feel that orthodox religion has let them down." Another American witch, Mrs. Raymond Buckland, is quoted as saying that she turned to witchcraft in search of a "spiritual experience."[6]

I do not presume to judge the spiritual depth of any of the movements mentioned. I am concerned to point out the scope of the search for meaningful spiritual encounter in the new man. The new man is basically a spiritual man, but he wants his spiritual experience firsthand, not handed down through another. So he goes in search of a deeper reality and vitality which he can experience in his own feelings, a search for the ultimate in life, which some of us call God.

Given the chance, he might word it like this:

I have deep spiritual hungers which are not being met in the traditional churches I have gone to. I yearn for an experience of the deeper realities, contact with the ultimate, awareness of the eternal. I look to spiritualism, yoga, sensitivity training or anywhere else I can find this truth.

Notes to 11) Spiritual Man

1   Frank K. Kelly, "The Possibilities of Transformation,"
    Saturday Review, March 7, 1970, p. 17.
2   J. Oscar Frenette, "Quest for Mystique #2," radio broad-
    cast, WJR, Detroit, Michigan, January 1970.
3   *New York Times* News Service, November 27, 1969.
4   Ibid.
5   *New York Times,* October 31, 1969, p. 50.
6   Ibid.

There is a revolution coming. It will not be like revolutions of the past. It will originate with the individual and with culture, and it will change the political structure only as its final act. It will not require violence to succeed, and it cannot be successfully resisted by violence. It is now spreading with amazing rapidity, and already our laws, institutions and social structure are changing in consequence. It promises a higher reason, a more human community, and a new and liberated individual. Its ultimate creation will be a new and enduring wholeness and beauty—a renewed relationship of man to himself, to other men, to society, to nature, and to the land.[1]

Charles A. Reich

Through the centuries life has become an increasingly heavy burden for Man the Species, just as it does for Man the Individual as the years pass. The modern world, with its prodigious growth of complexity, weighs incomparably more heavily upon the shoulders of our generation than did the ancient world upon the shoulders of our forebears. Have you never felt that this added load needs to be compensated for by an added passion, a new sense of purpose? To my mind, this is what is "providentially" arising to sustain our courage—the hope, the belief that some immense fulfillment lies ahead of us.[2]

Pierre Teilhard de Chardin

12

Man
the
Unfinished

To claim, as I have throughout this volume, that there is a new species of man emerging, is also to make an immense assumption. If man may be evolving a higher form, then that claim rests upon the assumption that man is still evolving, indeed, that evolution is still in process, still happening —not complete, arrested, or stifled.

While I find many distinguished men of science today who are willing to affirm that man is still evolving, none give me more hope or confidence than Teilhard de Chardin. Teilhard is that rare combination of man who has not only worked with the raw data of the physical earth—the fossils, the implements, the bones of primitive man—but has worked at the highest level with the ideas and concepts and meanings of the data of evolution.

Teilhard has affirmed that man is still evolving, and that evolution in the lesser animals has leveled off. The full thrust of the evolutionary energy is now concentrated in the consciousness of man, the one animal capable of reflecting upon himself and his place in the universe.

If we are to find a definitive answer to the question of the entitative progress of the Universe we must do so by adopting the least favourable position—that is to say, by envisaging a world whose evolutionary capacity is *concentrated upon* and *confined to* the human soul. The question of whether the Universe is still developing then becomes a matter of deciding whether the human spirit is still in process of evolution. To this I reply unhesitatingly, "Yes, it is." The nature of Man is in the full flood of entitative change. . . . We shall then see that a vast evolutionary process is in ceaseless operation around us, but that it is situated within the sphere of consciousness (and collective consciousness).[3]

Teilhard believes that man is still at a primitive stage of his development. While man today is far superior to primitive man, in the future he will become increasingly conscious of his place in the universe. Teilhard sees man motivated by love, which infuses all life, moving toward an increasingly interdependent existence with all other human beings.

What we see taking place in the world today is not merely the multiplication of *men* but the continued shaping of *Man*. Man, that is to say, is not yet zoologically mature. Psychologically he has not spoken his last word. In one form or another something ultra-human is being born which, through the direct or indirect effect of socialization, cannot fail to make its appearance in the near future; a future that is not simply the unfolding of Time, but which is being constructed in advance of us. . . . Here is a vision which Man, we may be sure, having first glimpsed it in our day, will never lose sight of.[4]

My conviction that there is a new man emerging is based primarily upon my intuition and my interpretation of the events and currents around me. To be sure, I have tested that conviction with many people and found documentation for my feelings in many places. But it is reassuring to find a great scientist-philosopher like Teilhard affirming the possibility of a new evolutionary stage of man and expressing tremendous hope in man's future.

But Teilhard does not stand alone. I tested the idea of the new man emerging with several contemporary scientific thinkers. At the beginning of this section of the book, I quoted Robert T. Francoeur, a research biologist and author of such books as *Man and Evolution*. Dr. Francoeur says very simply that "a new type of human being is emerging today." In concert with other scientists, he is acutely aware of the degree to which man is capable of influencing his own future evolution through scientific knowledge.

Another noted scientist who has made this point is Dr. Jose M. R. Delgado, research professor of physiology at the Yale University School of Medicine. Delgado has done pioneering research with the human brain and how feelings and behavior may be influenced by electric stimulation. According to Delgado, we need to center our scientific research more on the study of mental activities. "There is a sense of urgency in this redirection because the most important problem of our present age is the reorganization of man's social relations." He emphasizes the importance of discovering the neurophysiological mechanisms which will help us understand human emotions and help us educate ourselves into "more sociable and less cruel human beings."[5] He again stresses education as the key to man's evolutionary future:

This is the process by which civilization will gradually be replaced by psychocivilization, representing a new step in the evolution of mankind in which technology and intelligence cooperate to reshape the structures and function of the human mind.[6]

Dr. Richard E. Farson, vice-president for Ecological Affairs and dean of the School of Design at the California Institute of the Arts, has stated very cogently the idea that man can influence his own future:

Mankind can rely on people as a resource for much more than is possible to imagine. It's really quite difficult to find the ceiling of what people can do for themselves and each other, given the opportunity.

The great frontier today is the exploration of the human potential, man's seemingly limitless ability to adapt, to grow, to invent his own destiny. There is much to learn, but we already know this: the future need not happen to us; we can make it happen.[7]

As we learn more and more about our amazing bodily mechanism, as we learn how to live without war, and as we become increasingly aware of our belonging to one another, we will become more and more able to influence our environment and social climate for the common good.

Man today is unfinished. Still evolving. Still to grow, change, expand his horizons. The new man emerging is not the complete, perfect, finished product either, but another stage along the way in man's continuing development. He, too, is Man the Unfinished. Man in Process. Man becoming fully and truly himself.

Notes to 12) Man the Unfinished

1 Charles A. Reich, *The Greening of America* (New York: Random House, 1970), p. 4.
2 Pierre Teilhard de Chardin, *The Future of Man*, tr. Norman Denny (New York: Harper & Row, 1964), p. 117.
3 Ibid., p. 15.
4 Ibid., pp. 262–63.
5 Jose M. R. Delgado, "Evolution of Physical Control of the Brain," the James Arthur Lecture on the Evolution of the Human Brain. The American Museum of Natural History, 1965, p. 46.
6 Jose M. R. Delgado, "Brain Technology and Psychocivilization," *Human Values and Advancing Technology*, comp. Cameron P. Hall.
7 Richard E. Farson, "How Could Anything That Feels So Bad Be So Good?" *Saturday Review*, September 6, 1969, p. 48.

Celebrate
the New Man

When the moon is in the seventh house
And Jupiter aligns with Mars,
Then peace will guide the planets
And love will steer the stars
This is the dawning of the Age of Aquarius . . .

from *Hair*

In each of us, now that we know so much and know how
little that is, there are two states of being, embracing and
struggling: Mankind I and Mankind II. We are still attached
to the earth, but our minds move in and out in a dizzying
rhythm. We are changing so swiftly that we do not know
what we are or what we may become.

Since Hiroshima, we have known that the old man must
die. The man of devouring ambition, the consuming man,
must give way to the new man, the learning man, the man
of understanding, the servant of life. The future depends
upon our opening of ourselves to the emergence of the
servant.[1]

Frank K. Kelly

In the preceding pages I have made a rather fantastic claim. I have insisted that a new man is evolving and beginning to appear in our midst. I have further claimed that we can recognize qualities of this new man in ourselves and in others, that we can sense his presence and feel his impact. If this is really true, then it is cause for great rejoicing and genuine hope for the world. In my inmost feelings, I know it is true, and I only hope you can begin to believe it too.

If the claim is true, and if it is to be given serious consideration, then there are some questions which need to be faced. I will try to address myself to those questions in this closing section.

Why Now?

You might well ask the question I have heard from time to time, "What makes you think there is a new man appearing *now?* Hasn't there always been a new man in every generation? Can't you find these characteristics in lots of people throughout history? So what's new?"

The question is legitimate. I believe we can see the emergence of this new man in great historical figures like Jesus and St. Francis and many others. He hasn't just appeared overnight. But there is a difference in the scope and extent of the new man. He is beginning to appear here and there all over the world. He is not the great exceptional figure

"I'm 33 years old and feel that I know this new man. To some degree I feel I'm a part of him. Many people in our church are frightened by him."

"Theoretically I like him and admire him, but practically I seem to be apart from him and emotionally I tend to reject him."

"The new man will be the force that can save our world from the disaster it is heading for—if there are enough of them."

"I've got two in my house, and he and she are both fascinating and frustrating. But fun."

"He attracts and frightens me."

"Yes, he is real, he is here—will there be enough of him soon enough?"

"I believe in him and long to be one myself. Believe that only in this new man is there hope of a change in our world."

"I like the qualities that you say are a part of the new man. I am 27 and feel that I am acquainted with a limited number of persons who really are this new man. These persons are younger than me. I believe strongly in persons having dialogue and becoming involved in what they believe. Since I am out of school I find this is hard for me to do. Other ladies my age do not share my ideas and I do not have the strength to go out on a limb by myself."

"I think the 'new man' is the best thing that has happened to the human race! I feel like you have described me personally—but I hadn't thought of myself as a 'new man'—I considered myself *rebellious;* but like the term 'new man' much better."

"I think the 'new man' is a much more whole creature who has a greater ability to appreciate many more facets of life than his predecessors."

any longer; he is becoming the common man. And to speak to the question *why*, I would like to suggest briefly seven factors which are creating the pressure and the atmosphere for the emergence of the new man at this time.

1.) Perhaps the deepest and most ultimate cause for the new man's emergence now lies in the movement of history and the process of evolution. As Teilhard de Chardin has argued so brilliantly, we are witnessing the evolution of a collective human consciousness. According to Teilhard, there is a basic thrust, the spirit of love, present in every living cell. This common element in all forms of life and all humans is drawing us inexorably together in cooperation and common cause.

The evolutionary thrust is now concentrated in man, and is being expressed in spiritual growth rather than physical mutations. Our human awareness is expanding to include others, aided by the necessity of cooperation brought on by population increases and other world pressures.

To put this idea in different language, there is a providential dimension in man's pilgrimage, a leading that beckons us on to something higher and better than we now have. Because of my personal theological background, I call that the work of God in history.

2.) The new man may also be emerging in response to the pressure of our technological advances. Our technology has helped create a massive pollution problem, but there are hopeful signs as I write this that public apathy is being replaced by concerned action to save the planet. The pressure of the hydrogen bomb and its awe-inspiring threat is also forcing us to begin listening to each other across international lines. We now know that we must get along or we will all be destroyed. A few years ago writers were speaking of the gap between our technology, our scientific know-how, and our spiritual capacity as human beings. Technology had leaped ahead and man didn't know how to handle the resulting problems. Today, he is beginning to leap ahead morally and spiritually to catch up with that technological leap. He must leap or die, and he has chosen to leap.

3.) If we take Marshall McLuhan seriously, and it is difficult not to, then we must recognize the impact television is having on us. As a medium of communication, television is influencing the sense ratios in man, and changing the ways in which he perceives truth and reality, according to McLuhan. He is no longer a man of books and the written word, but has become a participative creature who wants to be involved, just as television involves him in the creation of the message. If television is really changing us, then we may be in the process of becoming new men partially due to its impact.

4.) Apart from the electronic structure of television as a medium, the content of television also has some effect on our ideas and attitudes. The honesty of the mass media at moments in relating the horrors of our present civilization has revealed our own hypocrisy to us. I *saw* the flagrant brutality of the Chicago police during the 1968 Democratic convention as they beat up the youth of America, including some I know and love. *My niece* had her arm broken by the Chicago police, and even I can handle her without a club. I saw a South Vietnamese soldier on a television newscast stab a Vietcong prisoner of war in the back as he lay helpless on the ground. I saw the American military "advisor" make no visible protest to this inhuman act recorded dramatically on film. This occasional honesty of the media, even when accidental, is blowing the myth that we are the "good guys" on the white horses. We are being forced to look at ourselves in the mirror of human honesty, and we don't always like what we see. This new honesty is another factor in the emergence of the new man, the authentic concerned man.

5.) The insights from depth psychology have surely aided the emergence of authentic human existence, and must be considered one of the factors in the new man's appearance. As we have learned more about ourselves and what motivates us, it has become increasingly difficult to hide from our own hypocrisies and self-deceptions, and this has freed us to become more real. Adjunct to the growth of psychological knowledge is the rise of the human potential movement as a trend within psychology. Many workers with people now stress what man can do, not what he shouldn't have done. They help us establish goals for ourselves, stretch our horizons, hope for a future. They help us heighten our awareness of beauty and pain and joy, and the new man is in some respects a response to this affirmation of his potential.

6.) The fact of widespread opportunities in adult education may also be a factor in the new man's appearance. Housewives may now study oil painting or sculpture or current political trends by taking a few hours in the evening or spending a weekend at a workshop. The old view that education ends with formal schooling is now being replaced with a view of education as a lifelong process, so people respond by continuing to grow and learn.

7.) The appearance of birth control methods may also be understood as a factor in the new man's emergence. People are developing healthier attitudes toward their sexuality because they no longer need to see sex as something to fear. The possibility of conceiving an unwanted child is becoming lessened, so that two persons in love can make responsible decisions about their intimate life together in freedom rather than out of fear and dread.

Many other influences have contributed to the emergence of the new man at this point in history. Rapid transportation, space travel, electronic communication, all these and many more could be elaborated. Perhaps it is enough to say that there seems to be a response to the accumulated pressure of these factors which is beginning to change the style of human behavior.

The real question before us is whether the new man will emerge in time to save us from self-destruction. We are clearly in a race with ourselves. We have only a few years to reverse the pollution of our atmosphere and our waters, or we will choke ourselves to death. We have only a few years to bring our population problem under control, or we will starve ourselves. We have a moment by moment reprieve from atomic destruction until we can find how to live together in peace.

There is hope. There is a future. There is a new day dawning and a new man coming. Whether we win the race with our own destructive tendencies is up to us. We have all the tools.

Communicating with the New Man

If there really is a new man appearing in our midst, how do we communicate with him? This is not merely an academic question. As the new man arises and challenges our style of life, our institutions, our educational system, our churches, our courts, we must learn to understand him and to live with him. In short, we must learn how to be in communication with him in order to minimize the friction that can ignite open rebellion and further conflict *and* in order to learn from him the valid truth that he represents as well.

Communication, if it is real, works both ways, of course.

The new man also needs to understand and empathize with the humanness of those of us who are not as "new" as he is. I offer a few generalizations which may be useful as guidelines for communication between the new man and those of us with whom he must live.

The first guideline is how *not* to communicate with the new man. We do not communicate with the new man via the Nixon-Agnew approach or the Ronald Reagan approach. We do not open channels of understanding through condemnation or punishment or name-calling or loud insistence that our way is the right way and his the wrong. This only convinces the new man that he has not been heard, and of course he is right. The self-righteousness of this one-sided approach to communication leads only to further distrust, heightened frustration, and potential violence.

We do not communicate with the new man by establishing new dogmas or decreeing absolute positions on issues. He does not respond when lectured at or preached to. He simply withdraws and charts his course independently. The Roman Catholic Church should have learned this from the way in which the Vatican handled the problem of birth control. By issuing dogmatic proclamations, the Church probably stiffened resistance to their view and probably changed few minds. Millions of Catholics apparently continue to be guided by their own conscience in the matter of birth control, expressing their "new-man-ness" by defying the central authority of their Church. By trying to deal with the issue through dogma, the Church failed to really listen so their constituents could participate in a highly personal decision about their own lives. By failing to listen, the Church guaranteed that it would not be heard, at least by many.

I read an incredible newspaper column recently in which the writer ridicules young people who wear long hair.[2] He cites a reference, invoking the name of a famous child psychologist, saying that a fixation on hair is the mark of a fourteen-year-old. To the writer of the column, this proves that today's youth have undergone a "tremendous emotional slippage" and are all acting like fourteen-year-olds! The slippage is not in our youth; it's in the sneering, ridiculing rigidity of adults like this columnist who has failed to listen to youth. He has made a ridiculous intellectual leap by assuming that all young people with long hair also have a "fixation" on hair. He has also failed to listen to the long-haired youth in order to understand what their Samsonlike tresses really mean to them. Whenever we dismiss those who are different from us by ridiculous rationalizations such as this writer has made, we can hardly blame them for feeling disgusted.

We *do not communicate with the new man* by dogmas, decrees, condemnations, punishment, or insisting on conformity to an old way of doing things. We are simply turning him off and increasing the gap between us.

How, then, do we communicate with the new man? The key words are *listening, participation, involvement, touch, contact.*

We communicate with him first by listening, not speaking or telling or ordering. We begin with listening deeply, weighing, checking, asking for more detail and clarification, pondering, and trying to feel into the meanings of the other. So much of our listening is really an impatient waiting for another turn to speak, while the words of the other flow past us uncomprehended. When our turn comes and we make our next speech, the other person knows we haven't listened when our words reveal that we have not heard him. Genuine listening is sacramental and healing. When we demonstrate that we are capable of listening, we have earned the right to speak. (This principle applies to both parties in the game, not just one.)

We communicate with the new man by getting in touch with him, physical touch, making contact, feeling the communication of his hands, his eyes, his face, his posture, and letting him feel the reality of our physical communication. It is harder for two people to be enemies if they are in touch.

I saw this demonstrated dramatically a few days ago. I led a workshop for pastors and laymen on conflict in the church. I introduced a simple simulation game devised for the occasion, in which the group was divided into two "teams" taking opposite positions on the Vietnam War issue. As the teams chose a name to represent them, a nickname for their opponents, and as they presented their case and responded to the other team's presentation, some amazing things happened.

An atmosphere of suspicion emerged, rudeness and name-calling began, individuals were ridiculed, and emotional arguments prevailed over rational statements. After we discussed what had happened, I asked the two "hostile" teams to line up facing each other. The two lines then moved toward each other until each person stood facing a partner from the "enemy" team. With eyes closed, they reached out their hands and made contact with their partners. In the next few minutes, they explored the space around them, pushed and fought, made up, played, then said goodbye—all without words.

In the course of this simple, ten-minute exercise, I saw hesitation, curiosity, wonder, delight, laughing, and closeness. As the partners discussed with each other what had happened and how they felt about it, I heard real listening and wrestling with meanings. The total picture was an amazing contrast to the distance, the hostility, the suspicion and the name-calling I had observed but a few minutes before.

Physical contact was an important dimension in freeing

this open communication between persons who had just been shouting each other down. When we touch the new man or the person of another color or the political enemy, feel the warmth of his hand and the reality of his presence, he is not nearly so frightening or alien. It becomes easier to see him as a fellow human like us and more difficult to put him in a box and call him uncomplimentary names. Man has always been a tactile man, but the new man is admitting this to himself afresh rather than denying it as our culture has been doing. We need to include the tactile whenever possible as we seek to communicate with the new man.

We communicate with the new man by giving him a voice and a share in shaping the decisions that affect him. He insists on this now, and we might as well open the doors before he knocks them down. When we give him a voice, as when we give students the right to help shape university policy, we discover that he responds with intelligence and balance and creativity most of the time. The truth is that we need him, just as he needs us. He is a participative man, and through granting him the right to a voice we discover that he has something to teach us, a contribution to make to our understanding and welfare. Communication with the new man is possible, desirable, and mutually beneficial.

We communicate with him also by "going there" with him, by trying some of the kooky (kooky to us) things that make up his life before dismissing them contemptuously without adequate information or experience of what they mean. We may need to try meditation—his way—before sneering at it as a pagan practice. We may need to listen—really listen deeply and with full attention—to the music of the Beatles until we feel the depth and beauty and life force that is in that music. Our ears and lives are tuned to a different frequency than his, but if we really try we can tune in with him enough to grasp what it is he means.

So long as we stand above a person, figuratively or literally, communication is minimized. I will illustrate this by referring to a dramatic incident which occurred once where I was teaching. A young man wandered into the building one day wearing a beard, unkempt in dress, and obviously in a daze. The caretaker approached him and asked what he wanted. The youth kept repeating that he was looking for Jane. He knew Jane was there somewhere and he was determined to find her. The caretaker told him there was no one there named Jane and he would have to leave. The youth refused, and the caretaker tried to grab his arm and usher him toward the door. A scuffle ensued, and the youth ended up sitting on the floor still refusing to leave until he had found Jane.

When I arrived at that moment, I instinctively sat down on the floor beside the bearded youth. I asked him quietly what I could do for him. I said I wanted to help. He was obviously under the influence of a drug, not fully aware of where he was or what he was doing. He explained that he knew Jane lived in this house and he wanted to see her before he left. I said I would be glad to show him the rooms and together we could see if Jane was there. He cooperated fully, and after looking into a number of rooms, he admitted that he must have made a mistake. He allowed me to have the police called and went willingly with them to receive the help he needed.

I tried to enter into this bewildered young man's world for those few minutes by assuming his posture in order to make contact with him. It might not have worked had he been more "out of it" or more violent, but in his semi-conscious state, my identification with him permitted some communication.

The new man is not walking about in a drugged state, hopefully, nor am I for a moment equating the bearded youth with the new man. But the principle holds for all communication, including that between youth and parents. When we can identify to some extent with the person we wish to reach, he can respond to our reaching out to him. When we approach him with bayonets drawn or stand above him with a club in our hands, we guarantee communication failure. To reach the new man, we may need to go there with him, sit in his place, feel into his world, and try to grasp his meaning alongside him. This may mean some discomfort and some risk on our part, but communication always involves risk.

If you would communicate with the new man, you might try sharing honestly and deeply of yourself and your feelings. It may be painful to you to risk your self-image with honesty like that; but he will respect the honesty more than the phony self-image.

You communicate with the new man by recognizing and freeing the new man within yourself. When you feel and confess to your own honest impulses to be a free, authentic person, you cannot help but be open to that same quality in another. If you can wear sideburns yourself, you are more likely to understand another man's beard. Freeing the new man within means risk, openness, effort. It's scary. And exciting. And worth a try.

How Must Structures Change?

If there really is a new man emerging, then there will need to be changes in our social structures to accommodate him. The structures will need to change if man is actually becoming open, tactile, dialogical, participative. The structures now are created to provide for a more passive, meek, rigid, prejudiced, verbal, limited human species (which is you—and me).

If man is increasingly dialogical, the Democratic Party will need to begin listening to him as it formulates policy and selects candidates. The Democratic Party listen to the new man? It may sound like a pipe dream, but the day will come when that reality will affect even the political parties. There were encouraging signs in 1968 that the new man might have a voice in the selection of the presidential candidates. The political debts won out, and the man with the most chips on the table picked up the prize, but the day will come when the people will insist on having more to say about whom they want to elect as their national leader.

Religious organizations likewise will need to accommodate to the new dialogical man or perish. The Roman Catholic bishops are discovering that there are ways they can listen to the legitimate contributions of their priests, and the priests are even beginning to listen to their laymen. New social structures such as local lay-clergy councils are beginning to appear. Protestant worship in a few places is allowing people to speak with each other, share insights, touch flowers, hold hands, become real, living, talking persons. There is some excitement in these new, experimental forms, as well as some fear in those who are threatened by change. Many people place their personal security in the repetition of forms, and even if the forms have lost their meaning, their loss is occasion for fear.

Educational structures, likewise, will need to change more drastically, for the new man is immediately repulsed by structures which try to subdue his creativity, kill his spirit of search and adventure, force him into a mold. He wants to do meaningful things, share his ideas, be treated like a full person with feelings as well as intellect. Similarly, teachers want more voice in what they are asked to teach, and parents and school boards must find new ways to honor the teachers' legitimate desire to participate more fully. The list could go on, but the idea is perhaps clear. All our social structures must be reexamined in the light of this new man.

Celebrate the New Man

That which seems strange, new, or different, often frightens us. The new man is no different in that respect. Our common reaction is often to reject him, ignore him, punish him, or ridicule him. At the same time, he fascinates us. We envy his freedom, his honesty, his directness, and we wish we could be like him. These feelings of fear and fascination mingle in us, leaving us unsure how to respond to the new man. There is, too often, a tendency to go along with the hostile people who would crucify the standout, the one who dares to be different.

Of course, Jesus was the new man. He declared himself free of the rigidity of the law; he said that the law was made to serve man, not man for the law. He was free, but didn't use that freedom irresponsibly. He was free, but he loved and listened and cared and sacrificed for the sake of others. He was honest in his denunciation of those structures which inhibited humanity, he was open to hear the questions and answers of those who came to him, he encouraged the participation of all the people in feeding each other on the mountainside. He was deeply spiritual, but the temple was not the only place he prayed and found God.

This new man, this open, free man was rejected. He was liked too much! A really free man scares us. When I asked my audience to respond to the idea of the new man on one occasion, an adult wrote: "He scares the he .. out of me. Frightens me, makes me mad. Challenges my personality, makes me angry." There is a wistfulness in this mixture of fright and challenge. We fear the new man because we would like to be him, to be like him, and maybe we don't dare. We think of too many reasons not to change. "What would Mom and Dad think? How about my boss? Would my wife be able to adjust? Do I have the guts to really be what I would like to be? Could I take it?" So we crucify him when he gets too close.

Perhaps the first step in understanding and accepting the new man is to recognize him in ourselves. The new man is in you! To some extent, this new world has changed you. You may have ignored it, denied it, refused to admit it, but you are changed, different, new. You may not wear your hair like a hippie, or carry protest signs, or wear beads, but you are to some extent this very moment the new man. You are part of the evolutionary stream, the emerging global consciousness, the flow of history. The new man is in me and in you and everyone around us. We can deny he is there, but we cannot change the fact.

If we can admit that the new man is in us to some extent, it may be easier to see that he is good. He brings us joy and excitement and hope. He is a breath of fresh, cool air on a still, hot day. He may appear in excessive form at times, but he is the hope of the world. Learn to appreciate him, listen to him, touch him, hear his music, feel his vibrations. You will discover he is not to be feared. The fear is our enemy—most of the time. As Pogo once said, "We have met the enemy—and they are us!"

If we can begin to see that the new man is a gift of God, we can begin to free the imprisoned new man within ourselves, without fearing that we will destroy ourselves. We may discover that we can be honored for our honesty, respected for our openness, even while some will be surprised and puzzled.

Free the new man within yourself! Don't go overboard and try to be something you are not. Just be your real self.

Try it on for size. See how it feels. It may lead to some pain, but that is also the path to joy, deep full joy.

Celebrate with me the new man. He is coming. He is here. He is emerging. And his coming is cause for great joy and great hope!

Notes to Celebrate the New Man

1 Frank K. Kelly, "The Possibilities of Transformation," *Saturday Review,* March 7, 1970, p. 17.
2 John Chamberlain, "Emotional Slippage at Root of Long Hair?" *Detroit News,* March 8, 1970, p. 2E.

ANTAR
AND THE
EAGLES

ANTAR
AND THE
EAGLES

WILLIAM MAYNE

Delacorte Press

Published by
Delacorte Press
Bantam Doubleday Dell Publishing Group, Inc.
666 Fifth Avenue
New York, New York 10103

This edition was first published in Great Britain by Walker Books Ltd.

Library of Congress Cataloging in Publication Data

Mayne, William [date of birth]
    Antar and the eagles / William Mayne.
        p.   cm.
    Summary: Abducted and raised by eagles, a young boy is sent on a mission to rescue a lost egg and, in the process, save the race of eagles.
    ISBN 0-385-29977-X
    [1. Eagles—Fiction.   2. Feral children—Fiction.]   I. Title.
PZ7.M4736An   1990
[Fic]—dc20   89-34956
                                                                         CIP
                                                                         AC

Manufactured in the United States of America

March 1990

10 9 8 7 6 5 4 3 2 1

BG

For Mrs Smith's Top Table in the summer of 1988

Amanda Scarr

Diana Cloughton

Elizabeth Bell

Helen Lambert

because I expect them to stay top

1

Antar's little sister Roslin was taking a long time to settle the fowls for the night.

"She is talking to them," said Maray, their mother. "They are talking to her, and no one is going to roost. I shall fetch her in a little while, before she gets too dusty."

"I will fetch her now," said Antar. He was sitting beside the fire with his father, Aldect, and his mother, but wanted to go away. He did not like what they had been talking about.

"Sit down," said Aldect. "You must listen to what we say."

Antar did not want to listen. He did not want to hear about anything different from what he knew already.

"We have all had to do it," said Maray.

"My friends in the town are not having to do it," said Antar.

"If they were my sons they would," said Aldect.

"Then all of us would not like it," said Antar.

They were talking about going to school, now that Antar was about six years old. Antar had seen the school.

It had a high fence round it, higher than the fence round the hen-run. "You cannot see out," he said. "I do not want to be locked in there all day. And the schoolteacher is entirely like a pecking hen."

"What is that child doing?" said Maray, getting up and opening the yard door.

"If you do not go to school then you will not learn reading and writing and figuring," said Aldect. "I want you to learn them, and then work with me. If you do not, then I shall find the best boy at the school, and you will have nothing to do when you are grown up."

"I do not wish to do anything," said Antar.

"That is foolishness," said Aldect. "If you have not enough sense to go to school, then that is another matter entirely."

"I have enough sense," said Antar. "Already. I could work for you now."

Aldect built the high roofs of houses all over the town. He had put the smooth lead on the Town Hall, laying it sleek and shining over the yellow woodwork, like the scales on a lizard. He had slated the cottages down by the bridge, straight as print. Just now he was working across the green on the church, putting wood and lead on the spire, rebuilding the great ball on top, and making the cross above that bright and golden once again.

"I will not allow you up a ladder until you know reading and writing and figuring," said his father.

Only the day before Maray had had to help Antar down from a stool he had stood on to reach a high shelf. He had not been able to look down or climb down, and the kitchen had begun to sway about. He was glad that not going to school would keep him from ladders. What his father thought made no difference to that.

But there was no time to argue now. From down the

yard at the back of the house there came a long shriek, as if some dreadful thing had happened.

"It is your mother," said Aldect. And they both ran out of the house and through the yard, to see what the trouble was.

They saw the gate to the hen-run as soon as they had passed the stack of slates and the pile of drain-pipes, and run round the two carts his father used. Maray was standing there, with Roslin in her arms, and they were both looking into the run.

"What is it?" shouted Aldect. "Is it foxes again?"

"It's a big black cockerel," Roslin shouted. "It thinked I was a worm. It looked at me all sorts of times."

"It flew away," said Maray. "I don't know what it was. It was huge. The fowls have all fallen over and dare not get up."

"Cockerels do not fly," said Aldect. "So this is all nonsense. Where is this bird?"

Maray looked up and pointed. Hanging in the air not far away there was a big dark bird, watching.

"It is children flying a kite," said Aldect.

"Ah," said Maray. But Roslin did not think so.

The dark thing in the sky moved its wings and flew up higher, in a circle over the house and yard. It opened its beak. Kites do not have beaks. It called out. Kites do not call out.

"I shall get my gun," said Aldect, running back to the house for it and bringing it out. Roslin covered her ears.

The bird swung in a bigger circle, out over the green and over the river, and in a wider one again, above the church and over the fields, on each turn going higher and higher. The sun shone against it and showed bronze feathers. When the gun pointed to the sky the bird was only a speck.

"It is looking for the mountains where eagles live,"

3

said Aldect. "It has become lost in a storm. If it comes back I shall shoot it. Has it taken any of our fowls?"

Roslin and Maray rounded the hens up, waking some of them from a dream of terror where they lay with their necks stretched out, blinking and gaping. But when they roosted they were all there, squabbling, and shuffling about to get into the right order. Only the hens know that order.

Aldect took the percussion cap from the gun, put it in his pouch, and hung the gun over the fire again.

Maray lit the candles, and it was time for bed.

In the morning the fowls had forgotten what the fuss was about and had laid eggs. Aldect pulled one of his carts across the green to the church, put up a ladder, and went up to the top of the tower.

The tower was crowned with scaffolding, made from poles and planks, standing like a square, leafless tree right up the spire and to the cross above the ball.

From inside the tower the church bell rang for services, and the clock sounded the hours. At the top Aldect and his men worked, sawing and hammering, and sometimes having a fire to melt lead.

At night Aldect came down and took the ladder away, so that no one could climb up. In the middle of the day, when the clock struck twelve, Maray took Aldect something to eat. He would come down the ladder, then climb up and eat on the scaffolding with his men. They would smoke their pipes, and start work again.

"Well now, Antar," said Maray one day, "you can take your father his dinner. When you get there call up to him, and he will come down."

"I am ready," said Antar. "I shall never climb the ladder."

"When the clock strikes twelve," said Maray.

"I do not know twelve," said Antar.

4

"It is when it strikes the most," said Maray. "At school you will learn twelve on the first day. On the last day you will learn a hundred. Today I shall tell you when to go."

Antar set out at the first stroke of twelve, was at the foot of the ladder before the last stroke, and called up to his father.

Aldect did not reply. Perhaps he had been waiting until he saw Maray crossing the green. Perhaps he had stopped hearing the time ringing out on the clock. Perhaps he did not hear Antar's voice. Somewhere up in the scaffolding he went on working, driving in broad clouts to hold the lead.

Antar leaned on the ladder. It was springy against his back. He looked at the ground. He wondered why he did not feel dizzy when he looked at his feet.

I shall be taller one day, he thought. What will it be like then? He put his right heel on the first rung, and stepped up backwards, until both heels were on it.

Then he did it again, so that he was two rungs up, and the ladder was more springy.

He shouted for his father to come for his dinner, but still no one heard. He thought of lifting himself up one more rung, but his heels would not do it because of all the space in front of him. They thought he might fall off into the sky.

He turned himself round on the ladder, with his back to the sky, his face to the tower, and felt both safe and daring.

He climbed another rung, and the ladder was resting against his body in the same places, as if he had not moved. The church wall was nearer, that was all. He tried to give another shout, but nothing happened.

Tap, tap, thud, went the hammers high up the steeple,

and each time the scaffolding shook and the ladder quivered.

Antar was thinking that he could climb ladders, after all, and did not need school and figuring to help him do it. It was only a matter of lifting a foot carefully, then moving his hands with just as much care, and not dropping the dinner in its cloth. The other leg came up of its own accord.

He did it about fifteen times. I am good at it, he decided. He did it five more times. It was not difficult, but it was hard work, and his legs were tired, not frightened. He passed the dream holes, the windows in the tower where the sound of bells came out. The bells inside were hunched up and silent. In a few more rungs he reached the bottom stage of the scaffolding.

Here Aldect had built a floor out of planks, so that the men could walk about. It was a narrow floor, running along the wall, but Antar was sure it was safe.

He climbed off the top of the ladder and stood on the planks.

He saw his feet. He saw the planks. Then he saw the gaps between the planks, and far, far below he saw the churchyard, with Roslin looking up at him with a small and distant face, and Maray just as small beside her.

All round him the tower began to sway, and voices to call. There was nothing here to hold on to—to one side there was the smooth stone of the tower, and to the other the empty sky. The wall of the tower wanted to push him away, and the sky wanted to drag him out. And he knew that if he knelt down he would fall through between the planks.

The scaffolding began to shake as well as sway. The shaking was real, but the swaying was in his eyes and head.

All at once he was being held strongly by his father's arms, and knew he was no longer in danger.

"You should have waited for me," said Aldect. "I am used to ladders. You are not."

"I am not frightened," said Antar, his voice wobbling with height.

"Of course not," said his father, taking the bundle of dinner and wiping Antar's cheeks dry of tears with the cloth. "Before I set you on your way down you must come higher still and see the view. You can do that, I know."

Antar could only do what he was told. Aldect took him to the next ladder and sent him up ahead, following close behind.

"Higher is no higher," said Aldect. "There is more to be seen, that is all, and down is only down and the least distance of all."

Halfway up the steeple, on a stage beside the sloping lead, Aldect sat to have his dinner, with Antar beside him. They saw on one side the sea glittering under the sun, and on the other the distant mountains, where the snow lay all summer. Below them all the town lay busy, not knowing it was being watched.

"Now you must go back to your mother," said Aldect. "I have not scolded you. When you finish school you may come to work with us on the towers. I know you will agree."

On the way down the long ladder to the ground Antar did not think at all about school, or about anything but letting his feet find the next firm rung. When he was on the ground, Maray shook her head at him, and Roslin gave him a look of admiration and reproach.

No one spoke about what he had done. But he thought very often of the far, free, open upper air of sea and mountain.

2

Now and then, going with Maray and Roslin to the market in the town, Antar saw the school. It stood down a side road, a black building with a high fence round it. There was nothing far and free about it.

"It is like a hen-run," he told Maray. "I do not want to go there."

"You are very stubborn," said Maray. "And you know nothing about it. A wise boy would wait and see."

But Antar thought he knew; his friends were not going to school, and they were just as wise, surely, and just the same age. Most of all, he had seen boys and girls coming from the school weeping because their hands had been hit with a strap.

"It is naughtiness," said Maray. "There is no need of it."

His father said, "You will be brave enough to bear the pain. Knowledge is not easily come by. There is pain in life."

I am feeling it now, thought Antar. I am hurting them, and it comes back and makes me sad. He looked at his hands, but no one had touched them. His pain was inside.

"I know I am right," he said to Roslin, because he had to speak to someone.

"You will get the slap," said Roslin, shaking her head mysteriously.

For a few more days school was not mentioned. Antar played on the green, or by the river with his friends. Aldect and his men climbed about in the scaffolding cage on the church steeple. The gilder came and began to clean the cross on top, waiting for a still day before putting on the gold itself.

"It is so fine and thin, much thinner than paper," said Aldect. "It will blow away in the wind; and if it is touched by hand it melts. Once in place, though, it stays for many years."

The gilding went on slowly, half a day at a time, and the cross grew slowly lighter and brighter, and began to be holding up the whole church.

"We shall finish with the scaffold in a week," said Aldect.

"I shall come and work on the next job," said Antar.

"You will go to school," said Aldect. "You must be man enough for that first. You will learn how to work out for us the weight of a roof and how many slates it will take, and what they will cost."

"Also," said Antar, "they will sting my fingers with the strap, and I do not wish to go."

Aldect laughed at that. "When you work you will hit your fingers with the hammer now and then," he said. "Also."

But Maray said, "This boy will not speak to his parents like that," and sent him to bed.

The next day she took him into the town for new clothes.

"You are out at the knee," she said, "and through at the elbow. Sunday is Trinity Sunday, and you will look fresh in church. The day after that, you can go smart to school."

The thought of school being so near made Antar unable to say anything except, "You will have to make me go."

"We shall," said Maray.

"I will go with you," said Roslin, "and look after the heavy slates." She knew there were slates on roofs, and slates in school, and thought they were just the same.

The clothes were stiff and new. The shirt collar stuck high against his ears, and the pattern was a thin red stripe on a brown herringbone. The trousers were blue, tucked into new black stockings, and held up with black shoulder-straps. There was a plain calico waistcoat with four pockets and eight buttons; there was a peaked cap, blue with a black band; there were new boots that would not let his foot in or out easily.

Maray gave the store all the money in her purse, and Antar carried the things home, proud but unwilling. They were the uniform of school, and he did not know how he could wear them.

On Sunday he put them on while the bells rang for the service at church. When he was dressed Maray stuck his hair down with cold water and a scratchy brush and told him to sit still while she dressed Roslin.

Aldect went across to the church to make things ready for the service, because he was an officer in there. People began to cross the green and come up from the town. The bells sounded over all the houses and echoed back from the high Town Hall. Roslin put her hands over her ears and Antar laughed at her.

"Go across to your father," said Maray. "You can help him. Roslin and I will follow soon."

Antar took his first walk in the new boots, clump over the doorstone, crunch across the gravelly path outside, and then quiet but heavy across the green. Once he kicked his own ankle. Once he took off the cap and settled it on his head again like any smart young man. He put his thumbs in his waistcoat pockets. He pulled up his stockings a little, and scratched his legs where the wool tickled.

He looked good, he thought, but there was no one there to see; and the clothes were for school as well. He hoped his friends did not shout at him.

He came to the church, with the bells still shouting high above. The church door was beyond the tower, round the corner of the building. Antar felt shy about going in alone, and waited a moment where he was.

He rested his hand on the ladder that went up to the scaffold. Aldect had not taken it away the night before; or perhaps he had been up the outside of the tower this morning. The ladder was here, anyway, going up past the dream holes into the sound of bells.

A new boot put itself on the first rung. Antar thought he was not doing it, that it was happening without any help from him. He remembered, too, that he was going to be very frightened.

I shall just go up and see the bells swinging, he told himself, or his boots, whichever was doing the walking.

He went up the ladder, five, nine, twelve rungs, and the boots were stiff and accurate; the thick leather soles seemed to hold the ladder better than his own feet last time he came here.

He slowed his climb after the fifteenth rung, and nearly set off down again. But he found the ladder was not in exactly the same place as last time, and he could not see so well into the dream holes. He remembered that the first level of staging went past them, because they were like tall windows. He climbed on. There was time to look and be down again before the bells stopped; and even when they did, the five-minute bell would ring for a long time. He did not know much about five, or about minutes.

He reached the staging and stood on the planks. He was out of breath and his heart ran about inside him, but he did not feel dizzy at all. There was no time for that.

He walked along the wall of the tower and looked in through the hole. Inside, the bells were heaving about like huge fish in a small pool, sending out noise in one everlasting beat. The bells did not sound better from close to, but a hammering jangle.

As well, the tower really swayed with the noise. It was not the swaying of height, but movement while the bells lifted and dropped in their chamber.

The everlasting beat would go on everlastingly, Antar thought. There was time to go down without any hurry at all.

But when he came to the ladder again, and wanted to start down it, some of the awful dizziness returned, and he could not turn his back on space to put his leg down and across to the top rung.

I will in a minute, he thought, and had another look at the bells. They had become too noisy now, and did not make him happy.

I will go up a little, he thought. I have been there before.

It was not difficult. He walked to the corner of the staging and went up the second ladder, out of the clamour of bell music.

He left the ladder and walked to the slope of the steeple, where he had sat with his father. The bells became peaceful below him, though they still rang, and though the steeple swayed with the tower.

12

There was another ladder here, climbing close against the lead, where the steeple grew narrow as it rose higher. Towards the top of it Antar could see out to either side. On his left hand was the sea, far away; to his right the mountains were high.

From this height the ground beyond the scaffold did not trouble him any more, because it was not below him but at the other side of the tower. The town, with its small buildings, was another world, like something upside down, all roof and yards and parts you do not see.

Still the bells rang under his feet, and the steeple moved under the noise. He climbed up and up, because this was a long ladder indeed.

He found he was alone in a strange way. First, the bells swung to a close and hung up their noise. Next, he was climbing a ladder with nothing round him, because he had come up beyond the scaffolding. There was only the steeple with the ladder against it, himself on the ladder, and nothing but distance between him and the town, him and the sea, him and the mountains. He was alone in the upper air, holding on with hands and feet.

He went on climbing. He stopped when he hit his head on something and almost let go.

It is the sky, he thought. I have reached it.

It was not, of course. He had come up under the ball at the top of the steeple, which was there in the style of his country. His head had bumped on the new lead.

He looked round him. Here at the top there was still scaffolding for the gilder to work from. Antar reached up a hand, found a pole, turned himself to one side, and was up in a framework that surrounded the ball. The poles were so close together it was like a ladder all over.

The five-minute bell began to ring below, chang, chang, chang, endlessly. Antar was so near the top he had to get there before he could turn round to come down again. In a moment he saw the gold corners of the partly gilded cross, and the dull metal not yet gilded and varnished.

It stood clear of the scaffolding, with a little platform all round it. It was taller than Antar but slimmer. He stood beside it and stretched out his arms to be like it, all freshly gilded himself, he thought, in new clothes.

He felt unsteady facing outwards, because there was a wind living up here, tugging and pushing. He faced the cross instead, but still stretched out his arms.

No one can be higher, he thought. But I must go down. I have been brave, and if they knew they would be pleased, perhaps; but now I must be braver, because going down is worse. I am only at the top because I dared not go down.

He had nearly finished this thought when he suddenly felt saved. Once more, now that he had got into a difficulty, he was held from behind by something strong.

This time it was not only a sudden tight grip, but it was not at all reassuring or friendly. It was as if a rope had been wound round his chest and waist three times and pulled tight. All his breath coughed from his body, he bent double, and lost his footing. The platform went away from his feet, and he was in the air.

Somewhere to right and left of him black patches came and went in the sky. He supposed it was the church tumbling past him. Then he saw, quite clearly, the church below him, the five-minute bell still clanging, Maray and Roslin walking across the green, and knew he was falling upwards.

Then a head, with a yellow eye and curved beak, looked down at him from above. The beak took hold of him by the new waistcoat, gripped and shook him, and the tight bands that held him shifted their grip from his

14

chest and waist to his hips and shoulders. The head went away again.

Antar knew he was being carried away towards the mountains by an eagle. The steady sweeping pulse of its wings bore him away from the town, away from the frantic calls of Maray, away from the summons of the five-minute bell, away from all he knew.

"I will go to school," he shouted to the eagle. "Take me back."

But the eagle flew purposefully along, the sky grew black and invisible, and Antar fainted away.

3

Antar came out of his swoon without knowing where he was. He was now being held so that he looked downwards at a stitched quilt, like the one on his bed but not the same. He wondered why he was breathing so heavily and so slowly, why his bed was so uncomfortable and why he was so cold. He thought the roof had come off the house.

Then he knew he had woken into a hideous dream, and found that it was true. The quilt below him was the ground, covered with fields and trees, with paths and roads threading their way across it, and the river lying like silk down the centre, not wet but flat, and in one place slashed with sunshine.

It was not his breathing that he heard, but the strokes of the eagle's wings, pulling the air in and out, and lifting, lifting, swinging in a wide circle to gain height. The landscape below swung the other way, tipping and tilting, sliding off to the left hand all the time.

The discomfort was not a hard bed but the talons of the eagle at his shoulders and across his hips. The cold was the high air itself, or perhaps terror, or the sweat of having fainted.

Antar turned his head, and saw from the edge of his eye the great bird sternly working its way along. It held on its way without hesitation, steady and determined. Its eye looked back at Antar with some purpose in it that he could not define.

Antar looked to the ground again, to one side and another. The bird circled out towards the sea, and half the world was water. It came back across the town, the house roofs ran away below, and the mountains held up the distant sky.

In the town and across the green, men and women were moving about. Antar could hear their voices, shouting, calling, in a great confusion. The church bell was ringing now, not the even strokes of the five-minute bell, but the hasty jangle of alarm, crashing across the land, pounding against the sky.

Before the noises faded there was another one that Antar knew. Someone had fired a gun. As the noise of it came to Antar he felt something pull at his shoulder and pass by snarling, and knew it was the bullet.

He felt the eagle shake in its flight, twitching all its muscles, losing way for a moment, then flying strongly on in a last circuit of the town.

Antar saw clearly the upturned faces of Roslin and Maray, outside the door of the house. They gazed upwards like two frail flowers. Roslin lifted up her arms to him, and Maray covered her face.

Now Antar was being taken towards the mountains in a direct line. He no longer saw the town, or could distinguish small objects, because he was too high up. The river dwindled to a brook, the roads to small tracks, and the paths vanished. Single trees looked like specks on the fields, and small groups like shadows. Woodland and for-

17

est were green like unformed fields. Ahead were the bare rock walls of the mountains, still a great way off.

Tears began to form like ice in his eyes. They were partly caused by the wind cutting at him as the eagle flew, and partly came up from his own misery at being where he was, caught by a wild animal and being carried to unknown places; and from leaving everything that was home. Mother, father, sister, house, town, church, were all suddenly not there. It was one thing to feel himself taken away from them, and it was another to know that they had helplessly watched him being carried off, and could not know what would happen to him.

These thoughts joined together to become unbearable. First there were tears in his eyes, and then he was crying.

He had to stop. Crying means sobbing, and sobbing means breathing in and out in a particular way. But sobbing was the most painful thing he could do now. His chest would not move, and he could only just breathe in any case. To sob was beyond him.

After a time even breathing seemed impossible, and he thought his back had broken.

Perhaps the bullet is in my shoulder, he thought. He could not bring his hand up to feel, however, because of the way he was held.

The flight went on. Antar did not know how to measure time in any case, only knowing that sometimes a minute was a long one and sometimes a short one. But he knew that men from the mountains came to the town market only once or twice a year, because it took a week to get there and back. He thought he might be flying for some of that time, day and night, sure he would die of being carried long before that.

The mountains were ahead, but Antar had no sense of getting nearer. It seemed to him that they were hanging in the air and not moving. The ground below remained

18

fixed when he looked at it. Only after he had looked away for a long time did it seem they might not be in the same place above it.

Then they were above the forests, and it was hard to tell one stretch from another. Antar found his eyes had dried. He tried to rub them with his hands, but could not get his fingers to reach. He could see them, and move them, and that was all.

He thought his legs had stopped working for ever and that he might be dying gradually. He hoped it would be soon, to take the pain from where the talons gripped him.

The eagle had stopped climbing the air now, and flew more slowly, its wings still scooping a space in the air ahead and driving it forward. Antar could distinguish the forward stroke from the backward one by sound, and could sense the change in movement. The forward stroke lifted him a little, and the backward stroke tipped him forward and down.

The gentle sound, and the small differences, made him sleepy. He thought he could not sleep, carried as he was, but he found he was waking gently from time to time.

One of those slumbers was ended by a different movement. The eagle had twitched again, in mid-flight, and broken the rhythm of its progress. For some reason it also clutched Antar more tightly still for a second, which both woke him up and almost took away his senses.

There were three or four more powerful strokes from the wings, and then the bird hung in the air, and glided. It was clear to Antar that they were gliding towards the ground, and that the mountains were still a long way off. So was the ground, for that matter; but the bird must be intending to land far short of the crags against the sky.

We are nearer, Antar thought. I can read the face of the mountains.

19

At that moment a drop of blood fell from the eagle on to his hand, lying like a crimson jewel, glistening on his skin. Past his hand, and sometimes striking it again, fell more drops of the same blood.

The eagle gave a sigh, quite unlike the sound of wing-strokes. It folded its wings to its sides, drooped its head, and closed its golden eye.

Antar was all at once without pain. The dreadful grip of the claws had been released, and he had his arms and legs again.

The eagle rustled all its plumage above him, opening its wings, trying to hold the air and lift again.

By now it was not gliding but falling, over and over, at first with its wings close to its sides, and then with them shaken loose and limply pulled about by the air. It tumbled and turned, its eyes closed, its beak parted, its talons curled up soft. It was plainly dead.

Antar fell beside it. He was glad for a short time that he was free of its clutches. Then he too began to be buffeted by the air and to tumble and turn. The sky and the ground, the mountains and the sea, the clouds and the trees, began to spin round and round him.

But always, he knew with a sudden new dread, he was in fact dropping down from the sky, and would shortly hit the ground. Whether it would hurt a great deal, or not at all, he knew it would happen. And he would be far from home, and perhaps never found.

So the two of them fell, Antar faster than the eagle, out of an empty sky. Antar knew that the only miracle would be for his father to be among the trees below, and catch him. At the same time he knew that was impossible.

4

Antar found he was trying to hold the air as it roared past him, but there was nothing to grasp. It was most urgent to take hold of something and save himself; but it was not possible. Air is too large and thin for a hand to clutch.

He continued to whirl and spin downwards, although the whole of the sky and the land seemed to be sometimes above him and sometimes below.

His cap left his head and floated beside him, then wandered away. He knew there would be trouble if he lost it.

He saw the mountains yawing and swaying at the edge of sight, and in the sky between him and them a flock of many birds, spread over a great distance, and calling out in harsh voices. Some were close and black, and coming towards him.

The wind that supported him shifted his hands and he somersaulted down the sky again, sickened and dizzied by the changes in his position, despairing of any help. Then he was lost among clouds, all at once blinded by mists so that he could not tell where he was or which way up.

As he came out into clear air again, with the shadows of afternoon streaking the ground below, he saw he was not alone. There were birds round him, flying as they dived beside him, flying with sweeping strokes of huge wings, watching with yellow eyes, hard and bright.

The eagles had come again for him.

In a moment more he knew he was to be killed before he hit the ground. He had felt pain before, when he was grasped by the waist, and then at his shoulders. But this time claws took one ankle and held him by it, so that he was not falling without weight, but hanging with all his weight from one limb. And that limb was held as hard as if a house had dropped on it.

On the other ankle there was a blow like a hammer, where an eagle struck with its beak.

Antar thought he was to be pecked to death, held by one leg. But the eagle was shifting the second ankle away from the first, so that it could hold it with its talons.

In a moment it did that. Antar found that he was hanging by the legs, and falling much more slowly, much more steadily, but still in pain from being held so tight.

In front of his eyes a third eagle slowed with a noisy filling of feathers. It had been power-diving, and now was adjusting to his speed, ready to hold him by the wrist. It took his left hand in an upward turn, pulling his arm up behind him, so that he was now lying in the air, face down, agony in three places.

From below a fourth bird rose at great speed, pecked his right wrist away from his face, where his hand had been, and grasped it in its claws. That arm too was twisted back and held.

Antar was supported by four eagles. Their wings began to work through the air with the noise he already knew, forward stroke and backward stroke, air through feathers, air held by them. The wings were so large that the birds had to stretch him out as far as they could in order to fly at all. Occasionally there was a rustle when their wings touched, and a small break in the flow of sound.

Their talons were locked into his wrists, giving two separate pains; both arms were twisted into shapes they had never been in before, and both felt as if they must break away from his shoulders. Both ankles were fixed through with nails, and he expected to split open where his legs joined and break into two, or probably four, pieces.

But he was no longer falling. He could see below him the eagle that had taken him from the tower, still tumbling like a bundle of rags. Now it was attended by a number of others, who gradually turned its twisting descent into a smooth path, and then began to hold and carry it, much as Antar was being held and carried. It was easier to carry, because its wings were so long and wide. One eagle took each end, and a third came down and took hold of the back, near the neck. In this way they managed to glide and soar.

The head of the shot eagle hung heavy on a limp neck.

Antar was not so far above the ground as he had been, and could see his progress across the forest. He found it difficult to look ahead because that meant raising his head. With such pain in his shoulders, his neck did not want to make the effort.

He and his eagles were going in the same direction all the time, he found. The sinking sun threw long shadows across clearings, and the shadows all lay across his path. But there came a time when there was only shadow below, and dark trees without any form or shape at all.

The wing-strokes above him began to slow, and the birds began to call. Antar did not know the reason. It was clear there were more birds round him. He expected now

23

to be held in more places, but in fact there was a change-over of birds to carry him. There was a quick release of one joint after another, then a fresh clamping as the cold claws of new talons held him in a slightly different place.

He was still supported, still being carried, and if the pain was no less it was no greater either.

After a long time with the ground invisibly black below him, something began to change. He could now see something of it again. The forest had been replaced by rocks and ground broken up into boulders and canyons. The rocks reflected light, but the spaces between were deep and dark.

The eagles sank towards the rocks, which were part of the mountains, close now, and above Antar. Beyond the rocks the side of the mountains stood like a tower, rising nearly sheer for thousands of feet. Nothing grew on the steep slope, and there was only a frail network of marks that might be goat paths.

The flying stopped. The wings became still and almost silent. The birds dropped from the air, still holding Antar, and set him down hard on a bare slant of rock.

They let go of him, and lifted themselves into the air again. Two of them dropped down to nearby pinnacles, where they perched and trimmed their feathers.

Antar could not perch. He could not grip anything because of the slope, and began to fall down it. His hands and feet would not work because his arms and legs were useless. He fumbled and tumbled, and rattled down the flank of the mountain whether he liked it or not.

He slowed, when he came to a flatter place, and there he sat, waiting for some good thing to happen, being still for the first time that day. He thought, I shall sit here until morning, and then go home. No. I shall go home now.

With his feet clumsy under him, his arms stiff like a

gate across his shoulders, he stood up in the dying sunshine, and began to run down the mountainside, towards a clump of trees.

When he did so all four eagles came and circled his head, so close he could not see where he was going.

He sprawled over the roots of a pine tree, and found himself among the branches touching the ground, lying in the needles. He wanted to cry out, but he had lost his breath. The eagles would not let him recover it.

Two of them came in under the trees with him. One stood on his right side, the other on his left. They turned him round, so that he was facing the nearest tree. They stabbed at the backs of his legs until he walked to the tree. They continued until he began to climb it.

He began in the dark, and ended up in the light again, with the sun still sending a sloping beam across the highest branches.

He climbed as high as he dared. But that was not enough for the eagles, who made him climb where it was not possible—unless eagles were stabbing at your heels.

At the end of the climb his new clothes were torn, with the shirt sleeves hanging in shreds, the blue trousers burst out at the knees, and the new boots scraped through to the white inner part of the leather so they would never shine again.

He was bleeding at hands and knees. His face was wet with heat, and he was filled with both hunger and a feeling of sickness.

He was quite without hope when he reached the feathery top of the tree. He clung there expecting he would die, if dying is a comfortable sleep where nothing goes wrong.

Eagles stood in the tops of other trees, seven or eight of them, balancing on an evening wind and stretching their wings out to stay there. One of them fixed its eye

25

and ear on something not far away. It did not speak, staying frozen until it left the tree all in one movement and one piece, and moved to another.

The rest of the birds were watching too. One by one they moved uneasily away, until they were in another circle some distance away. Antar felt abandoned and neglected by their behaviour.

He was thinking of leaving the tree and finding another that put him in the centre again, when he heard for himself what the eagles had sensed, that someone was coming that way. A man was whistling, while he walked through the forest.

"Help," said Antar. He said it first to the tree, which took no notice. Then he said it louder, and the whistler took no notice. Then he shouted it, and the whistling stopped.

"Who that?" asked the whistler. "What you doing here?"

Antar suddenly realized that he was safe. He would be in trouble for ruining his clothes, but the trouble would mean he was at home. He called out again, meaning to say he was Antar, and up a tree, and stolen by eagles. All that came from his throat was a wailing sob, quite unexpected, and a flood of tears that filled his nose and mouth. He snuffled and bubbled, blubbered and choked, and could not say a word.

"Who there?" asked the whistler again, in his woodland dialect. "If you bear I skin you."

"Me," said Antar; but he, and anyone hearing him, would know it was a screech.

Down in the darkness under the trees there was light where a fire had been brought to flame. Sappy pinesmoke drifted into Antar's eyes.

"I lose you," said the whistler. "Call another call."

The light moved about, being a torch of bark.

"I'm here," said Antar, getting his voice clear. "I'm up a tree. Please get me out."

His voice must have miscarried in some way, because the torch moved away, and the whistler called from further off. And there were other noises, as if other boys were in tree-tops. Antar could not understand them.

He thought he would climb down and find the whistler. When he was looking into the dusk round his boots the eagles came back. Four of them came close, took him first by the arms and lifted him into the air, then by the legs as well, and carried him off the tree.

By chance, this time they carried him on his back, which made breathing much easier and was much less painful. He saw the first stars beginning to appear like leaks in the sky. The steady pull of wings took him higher and higher. His arms and legs began to ache again, and he began to scream. He had no words to use now that he was being recaptured, and could not bear the horror of what was happening, and the thought that it could go on for ever.

Drawing breath between screams he heard the voice below calling to him.

"Antar," he shouted, suddenly able to do so. "It is Antar, carried away by eagles. Stop them, stop them, stop them."

For a short time he felt his words must have the right effect. Then it was clear they had not. The whistler could only shout, his voice growing fainter and further away as Antar was lifted towards the mountain again, going upwards to where the last of the sunlight still stood on the high snows.

5

A customer had once paid Antar's father with a double-bezant, a coin of the country. Antar had seen it, as big as the palm of his father's hand, clean gold right through, payment for the work of many months.

On one side had been a picture of a king long dead, though his money was still good. On the other, when Antar had been allowed to turn the heavy thing over, was a picture he did not at first understand. But when his father turned the coin round, because one side was upside down to the other, they all saw the picture of the spread eagle, wings stretched, legs extended, and the head lifted in pride. The coin had gone away to be saved or spent, but the picture stayed in Antar's mind. One day, he had decided, he would get two of them, and be rich for ever.

Now Antar did not think about being rich. He thought about being wretched, not the same at all. But here he was in the air, legs being pulled away, arms held out as far as they would go, spreadeagled in the sky. He would not be saved, he thought. Above him the eagles' feathers glinted in the sun, and their wings lofted him higher and higher, full of tawny light.

Antar was not comfortable, but he felt safe: these birds would not drop him from the sky on purpose, he was sure. Even the first eagle had not meant to do so; but when it died all it meant to do was lost.

Antar turned his head. He could look from side to side, and downwards as well. He was no longer being carried completely on his back, but in a sitting position without being bent. Down to one side, and lifting from the dark shadows of the ground, was a busy thing made up of eagles circling excitedly another close cluster of more eagles. This thing was made up of eagles carrying and escorting the first eagle, lifting and guarding, and coming the same way.

"Is it dead?" Antar asked.

His eagles opened and closed their beaks, but said nothing to him. A moment later one of those holding his wrists sent out a call that echoed and hung against the rocks of the mountains. From down below there was a reply, but Antar could not tell what it meant.

He bent his head to look at the other group, and he thought that his eagles swung their load to one side for a moment so that he could see better. Then they steadied their attitude again, and flew on, and up.

Antar's arms and legs stopped being there. Only his back still had feelings and twinges of pain, and those went away too. He went into a dream about being made of gold. Sleep and dream came to him together, and he knew that he had died and nothing could be done about it. Someone would find him, broad as a man's palm, one day, and spend him on something fine.

He woke, suddenly and alarmingly, into glimmering twilight and silence, the silence that follows the noise that woke you. He did not recall where he was for a

29

moment, and tried to move his arms. They were still held, and he knew the eagles were still there.

They were not now using wing-strokes, but hanging on an upcurrent of air close against the cliff of the mountain. The cliff still held heat from the day, and seemed to have some cast of light coming from it. The eagles circled in silence on the air's invisible tide, coming and going, dipping and rising.

They began to use their wings again, but found it difficult to fly together, because two of them were weary and were not able to lift. Also, Antar saw, they were no longer rising up the cliff but losing height. They continued trying to fly higher until some signal was exchanged with a little sound. They wheeled from the cliff, glided down, pulled up, slowing themselves on the air with cupped wings, and laid Antar gently on the ground in the dark.

He was lying quite still on a stony slope, on his back, with his head still swinging from the sky. The eagles let go of him, and stood aside, smoothing their wing feathers and stretching.

Antar could hardly move his legs, and his arms lay dead beside him. His limbs felt as if they were being hammered from inside, hurting so much that he was sure other people were there feeling the pain too.

The dead arms helped him sit up. The stones shifted under him. After a time he turned himself over on all fours, and knelt there with his head hanging. He was ready to escape but could not move.

When he was ready he stood up. That was a mistake. He had been brought down on to a scree, which is a slope covered with stones of about the same size. Left to themselves the stones sit there without much movement; but if someone, or an animal, tries to walk about, they slide underfoot. The walker then skids down the slope with stones rattling about his ankles, falls over, and slides even faster.

Antar did that. He went down the mountainside in a small but rattling avalanche, tumbling over and over, and ending against a large rock half covered with angry little stones, with more of them bounding down and rapping him hard and unexpectedly in tender places.

The eagles were extremely annoyed. They followed him down the slope and, one at a time fluttering over his head like windmills, pecked at his shoulders until he climbed the slope again.

Because of the ground he kept slithering down again. When he did so he had his back nipped, and his legs gripped with beaks.

"I can't help it," he shouted. "It's where you put me down. It's the ground sliding away, not me. It's not fair."

It was not fair, but it went on. Antar climbed until he was above the scuttling stones and on plain rock. Still the birds were not satisfied. He was not sliding down any more, but he was not climbing as they demanded.

They insisted that he went on climbing in the great darkness. Antar obeyed, hating the darkness, but hating the eagles even more. At least, he thought, I shall meet nothing worse. He clambered among boulders and crawled across cracks in the mountainside. Once he stopped, defying the birds, when water came tumbling cool and sweet down a cleft, to drink and splash water on his face.

He was refreshed by that, but hunger came into him then, and there was nothing to eat.

He climbed to a clean but steep slope of mountain, away from fallen and falling rock. There were pathways marked, where it was possible to walk. Sheep or goats or mountain antelope had been here, making the paths.

The hillside was so steep that the morsels of rock went

hurtling down, sometimes ringing and singing until they crashed against some rock a long way below, and smashed. Then their remains would rustle into tree-tops further down still.

The network of tracks followed the ease of the slope, and the eagles understood that. They wanted him to climb, but let him take the zig-zag way. If he slowed, or took a way they did not like, his ankles were hacked. He slowed too often, took the wrong track more times than he should, until his ankles bled.

The ground changed its nature in some way he could not detect. It grew more solid under his feet. No more fragments fell away as he moved. The air became very cold. A wind began to howl and grumble in crags nearby, dropping chill against him.

The ground became both hard and crumbly, and Antar could see it better. He understood what was happening. He was coming into the snow that lay on the upper parts of the range. At first there was frozen ground, then a scattered covering of snow worn thin by daylight and warm weather, then there was snow soft enough for his feet to go through and touch the ground below.

Next there was snow that had drifted deep, so that he walked in it and on it. It meant that he could kick holds for his feet as he went, and he did not slip downwards so readily. It meant too that he was going into places where he could not live, where there was nothing to eat.

Out of despair he found a friendly thought, without placing too much hope in it. The eagles, he fancied, were leading him to the warm hut of a shepherd, where there would be fire and safety, and a way home as soon as it was light. He toiled his way on, knowing it could not be true, but unable to hope for anything else. The eagles stayed close, hopping and flying across the snow, dark against faint white.

The snow vanished underfoot, there was complete darkness and a strange deadness of sound, as well as a flattening of the ground. Antar could stand upright and walk easily, and the wind had faded right away.

He walked, expecting his shepherd, or better. But he hit his head hard on overhanging rock and fell down. When he stood up he hit the rock again, even harder. The next time he felt the space first. There was an overhang, where snow had not filled the place underneath. There was rock above him and he could go no further.

The eagles thought otherwise. They gathered behind him, waiting and watching, while Antar fumbled and tumbled, finding nothing like a way forward.

He went along to the left, out from the overhang into the snow again, with the rock face standing straight up from the slope, quite unclimbable. He followed the foot of it until the slope he was on came to an end.

He knelt down to see where next to go, and put his head out over a cliff with no bottom, and a howling wind tried to drag him with it. He pulled back, because there was no way to go forward there.

In the other direction he did better. Beyond the overhang he found the same rising cliff, but cracked and creviced so that he could climb up. He did not want to, but the eagles snapped at his angles until he must. He climbed bare passages between slabs of stone, with snow crusting all the edges and handholds, until he came to something that was not rock.

He came across branches and twigs blocking his way. They made a solid barrier that could not be removed, as if a river had been depositing for years and years a deliberate wall of boughs and stems across the way. But he knew that could not be so unless a shepherd, perhaps, had made it.

The climbing was easier. Everything was firm to hold,

better even than a tree, and far better than rock. He pulled himself along and upwards.

Then he began to be uneasy, because he was turning on his back, because the thing he climbed had an overhang too.

He became aware of a smell of things old and rotten, like the dead bats his father once brought from a fallen roof. The smell, strong as smoke, choked at his throat. He was reminded of the hen-run at home.

Then he was climbing upright once again, hands ahead of him, feet clinging well to loops of wood and kicking into soft places.

He saw his hand again. It had gone up into a place full of light, and showed red, as if it had no skin on it. He was not surprised at that. He was glad too, to be coming to where the shepherd was, and his bright fire.

The rest of him reached the top of the climb and the light. He pulled himself up and knelt on the floor of twigs. He saw straight to the setting sun, miles and miles away, cut in two by the curve of the distant sea, and still shining on this high crag of the mountains.

Closer to him, and coming forward to him, was a group of hobgoblins with open mouths, shouting and crying out, their little arms with no hands spread, their ugly legs hurrying them along.

They were about to be busy with something, and Antar knew he was the thing.

6

The hobgoblins came clamouring towards Antar. He knew very well that he was now about to be eaten, but he wanted to know first why eagles were feeding hobgoblins.

He turned to go back the way he had come, because before knowing anything he wanted to stay alive, though he could not think it would be possible to climb down over the edge. He believed the eagles would drive him back if he tried.

He found them barring his escape at once, close behind him, standing with wings spread, great beaks like spikes across the way, feathers themselves like iron.

Overhead another rustling shadow fell from the air, and there were challenging calls and responses. The hobgoblins were making their own seething cries now, stretching their necks towards Antar.

He saw what they were. They had beaks gaping open, their short arms were wings without feathers, they were dressed in ragged down; and they were young eagles.

It is bad to be the food of anything. It is no better if what eats you is a brood of eagles. You end up eaten.

Antar was never sure afterwards whether he thought that all then, or added it to his memory later.

What happened next was confused, too. Something came out of the sky and began hurling things about. And at that moment the sun set entirely, leaving darkness.

The darkness was not complete, because the sky still glowed. Antar saw what was going on from the ground, or wherever he lay after being knocked down.

There was a fight among eagles, with a great deal of noise. None of them was being hurt badly, but there was a lot of stabbing with beaks, a lot of sword-play with them, and the shaking of wings, dancing on the spot in a threatening manner, and leaping into the air to come down on the back of another bird.

The young ones retreated from the scuffle. Antar crept to one side on all fours, moving off until his hand found the edge of the place, and at full stretch found nothing below. He nearly jumped, but dared not.

The row subsided. It had not been a fight among enemies, but a quarrel among neighbours. Before long six eagles stood in a circle and spoke among themselves in harsh and screaming tones, but without any more anger. Something had been decided by the conference.

Antar was brought back from the edge. He was put in the middle of the circle, and the four who had brought him here now gave him to the two that owned the nest.

Because he was, of course, in the nest of a pair of eagles, who lived here with their young ones.

In turn he was then put among the young ones, who pecked at him once or twice and had their heads pecked by their parents for doing so. They pecked at one another in just the same way.

He realized that he was not being eaten. He had not been brought here as a meal. He looked round from where he sat on hard and dirty sticks and twigs. The four young birds crouched down against him and their eyes were closed, bulging under their eyelids. The twelve eyes of the grown eagles looked at him, and they spoke.

He did not know what they said. He did not understand what had happened, or why. He knew that the birds had acted deliberately, and meant what they had done. They had kept him alive; they had not hurt him on purpose. But they had not explained anything.

Antar saw three of them lift away. One still stood at the edge as a guardian. Uneasily the pair that owned the nest settled for the night.

One of them arranged the young eagles in a convenient way and sat down on them. The other approached Antar cautiously, studied him with her beak, then arranged him conveniently too, curling him up and tucking him in, and she settled on him, spreading her feathers, stretching her wings, to wrap him from the cold of the night.

Antar was cold. He was hungry, thirsty, and choked by the stench of the nest, where rotting bones lay everywhere. He lay under the eagle and sobbed, full of despair, homesickness, sure he had done nothing to deserve this punishment.

He woke up cold. The eagle had left him while the daylight was still small. Her mate had left the young ones too, and they huddled together to keep warm. On the edge of the nest there still stood a sentinel, watching.

Antar got to his feet, then sat down again when the wind from the snow bit him. Also he had a feeling of height. In one direction lay the sea, very far off. In the other the forests ran misty into the distance. The sun behind clouds put a secret light into it all and made it impossible to see to the end. To one side the mountain went on up and up, with the snowline draped on its flank, blue in shadow, gold in sunlight, but never white.

To the other side there was a stretch of forest, then the distinct beginning of fields, where there would be people.

Antar saw he was on a crag, the best place for an eagle's nest, where the whole world was to be seen. And from any crag there is a way down.

Animals don't think of these things, he told himself. That one is standing where I came up. But I can go out on another side.

He found that he could, indeed, but that he did not want to. The edge had a straight drop, so far to the bottom that there were clouds hanging against the precipice half way down. Below the clouds, at the bottom, there seemed to be moss.

But those are trees, thought Antar, and felt a lurch inside him when he thought of the depth. There was no need to guard this side of the nest.

The next side was the same, where a ravine perhaps a mile deep dug back into the mountain. The bottom of it was still velvety darkness.

The fourth side was where the mountain rose in the same cliff, straight as a building and ten times higher. Down a crack there ran a trickle of water, melted from the snows. Antar drank from it, cupping his hands to bring the water to his face.

His wrists were scraped and bruised. The cuffs of his shirt sleeves were unpicked by talons and hung in shreds. His ankles were blackened with bruising and his new stockings full of holes.

Far below, the trickle of water he had drunk from grew into a fast river running straight downwards, and then into a mighty fall sending its loud roaring whisper up the cliff and through the rock.

The sentinel eagle turned its back on the nest and took the first rays of the rising sun. By turning its head it could see Antar. When he came near, hoping it would not see, it threatened him. It was ready to call for more help if it needed it.

"I just want to go home," said Antar, reasonably. "For breakfast."

The eagle did not know the words, but it understood, he thought. It wanted the same things itself. But it only turned round to face him, held on to the nest structure tightly, and lowered its head, ready to strike.

Antar went to the young ones. They looked at him with the wise but stupid look of young birds, and let him sit among them.

He was with the biggest eagles in the world, and these chicks were not much smaller than he was, though they were still without feathers. He felt warmer leaning against them.

They began to squabble and peck and climb on one another to get to the warmest places. When they pecked Antar he hit back with his fists. Under the down they were rigid with bone. He did not hurt them, and they did not make a fuss. Pecking and squawking were their ways of communicating. Antar joined in the squawking too, without knowing what the sounds meant.

The young birds fell silent together. They heard something Antar did not hear, and they began to wait for it, rising up and down on their claws, walking on the spot, doing a particular exercise with their wings, and getting their beaks to open and close. They were expecting something.

A parent bird came from the sky, hesitating, not quite understanding why there was a sentinel, wondering why there was a boy in the nest. Then she remembered and came down.

Antar knew the young ones were expecting food. He

expected some himself, now that he was part of the brood.

He was not sure what he would get, but he ought to have known. Eagles eat other animals, and so do people. The difference is that people cook their animals and serve them up clean.

Eagles serve their animals whole, and only just dead. The mother of this brood brought a mountain hare that had not moulted its winter coat and was still white. It had been struck and killed with its eyes open.

Antar was trampled in the rush to get the meat. He did not attempt to go near it, because he did not think of it as food. Food came in dishes. The hare was torn apart by the mother eagle, then eaten in gulps by the young ones.

Antar watched, unable to think of eating, yet not able to think of anything else. He did not think he could live on raw meat complete with fur, like the young eagles. There was no fur left after the meal. There was nothing left on the nest.

I shall die, he decided. Then they will let me go.

Another parent came, bringing a ground-squirrel with a striped tail. Before it could be broken up it had been swallowed by one chick in a slow gulp. The furry tail hung from the corner of its beak for a long time, twitching a little at first, then drooping.

I can't eat living things, thought Antar. Drinks of water will not be enough. I must escape.

Even thoughts of that became faint in his mind, because he could not remember anything about home. What was happening now was what filled his mind; and he did not know where home was.

Part way through the day the sentinel eagle was replaced by another just as watchful. Antar thought of escape as something you do before deciding where to escape to. His mind would not stretch further at all.

The sentinel would not stretch either. Antar found this eagle rougher than the first one, able to knock him down if he came near. He could not get past it.

I shall never know which one is which, he thought. They are all the same to look at, but this one has a different nature. We do not like one another.

He looked at it carefully. People look different, though they are all the same kind. Eagles must look different too. Already he knew things about the four chicks. One had a black ring round its eyes; another had yellower feet than the rest; another had wing coverts just beginning to goose-pimple through its wings; and the fourth was smaller than the others, had a weaker cry, and did not come to its food so quickly.

Grown eagles would be different too. He watched them as they came to the nest. He saw that the differences were mostly where the beaks joined the heads. The bronze colour of the feathers was in the beaks too, at that point, though the beaks were yellow after that. The pattern of the bronze colour was different in the birds he saw close-to that day. But it was not easy to remember.

And there were no names, because he could not tell what they were saying. Only the weakest chick had a name so far, because of its smaller voice. Antar called it Keek, the nearest he could come to a word from the sound it made.

Some of the day he spent asleep in the sun. He did not move about much because of his bruises and the stiffness of his back. And the day was long, with nothing to do.

But once there was something out across the mountain, where the precipice turned less severe. Across there, out of earshot, a group of eagles was moving another and a larger one slowly up the mountain, pulling and lifting, pushing and helping.

Antar thought it was the eagle that took him first, and

41

that it was not dead. It was a sign that the eagles worked together, not just in hunting (when they had herded Antar along) but in errands of mercy—they were surely rescuing the largest eagle out of kindness.

The father eagle brought an animal of a kind Antar did not know, brown with a dark streak and pointed ears.

It was not dead. The chicks pecked at it. It ran away and jumped over the cliff. That was all that Antar had on this first day.

7

During the night the mountains grumbled. Antar felt them shake and move. He heard the cataract far below hesitate and fail for a long time, then flow again.

He put his head out from under the feathers of the mother eagle, where he lay tonight with the chicks. He saw the sky turning black where the mountains covered it. He saw a star wandering on the mountainside, and did not know what it was.

He smelt a choking smoke drifting across the air. The mother eagle sensed it too, and stirred. The eagle chicks gabbled and fluttered under her, until she put her head down to see they were safe. She pulled Antar in firmly under her and settled on him again, pushing his head behind one of her legs. There he had to stay. The vibrations of the mountain still sounded through his bones, and distantly he thought he heard the star bounce and crackle down a slope.

With the first light the mother eagle had gone hunting. Antar lay uncovered, with the night's cold plucking at him. The young eagles huddled round him, waiting for food. At the edge of the nest another eagle stood like a sentinel, watching Antar. From the markings on its beak Antar was sure it was one of the four that had carried him and then chivvied him up the mountain. He felt certain that one of the four always stood at the edge of the nest.

When food came there was more than the usual commotion. The young ones always bickered and pecked, and they began with this meal. The meal was a small mountain antelope, its neck broken by the weight and talons of the mother eagle. She dropped the warm body on the nest, then stood by for a moment to put a few feathers in place.

The sentinel eagle spoke. The mother eagle replied. Antar, of course, could not understand any meaning, and thought there were no words. The mother eagle got ready to fly again.

The sentinel came forward into the middle of the nest. The mother eagle shouted at him and spread her wings in threat.

The young eagles were beginning to break the skin of the antelope. The smallest one pecked at its eyes. Antar thought that he could eat meat, even raw, but he saw there was no way of getting any. The beaks of the young ones were not long, but they were sharp. Antar had nothing but bare hands.

The sentinel eagle pushed his way to the antelope, ripped skin off it, scattered the young ones, and pulled a gobbet of flesh from the back of the animal.

The mother eagle was not standing for that. With a shriek she came half running, half flying, at the sentinel. She did not like other birds near her nest at any time, and this one was not allowed to take food from her family.

She called out, and there was an answering cry from her husband, circling a peak half a mile away. He came

44

flying back as fast as eagle can go, ready to fight off invaders.

There were shouts and squalls, and three birds bristling their feathers on the nest, flapping wings and parading towards each other.

The young ones went back to the carcase. The sentinel brought his piece of meat and stood in front of Antar with it.

He wanted Antar's beak to open, so that he could put the meat in. The parent eagles understood what was going on, but felt it was so wrong they could not allow it. As well as that, it was plain that they knew they had to allow it. They walked back and forth indignantly, scolding and rustling.

Antar thought they were like the schoolteacher at the school. He had only heard of her, but that was how she was reported.

It was like having three schoolteachers. Antar was the one knowing nothing, not understanding what he should do, unable to get the meat from the bird. When he politely stretched up his hands they were knocked aside. Eagles know perfectly well that you do not eat with your wings.

In the end he had to open his mouth and wait. The huge beak came swiftly close to his face. Then the meat was rammed into his mouth and pushed hard back. Antar began to choke. The sentinel went back to his watching post, and watched.

Antar pulled the meat from his mouth and held it in his hand. His mouth was stretched, and his throat had been made to feel sick. But he needed food, and this lump was it.

He tried to bite a piece off it. His little teeth were not sharp enough for the job, and in fact one of them came out as he chewed. But the others raked off some fibres,

45

and his mouth began to moisten inside when he tasted them.

He swallowed the first scrapings. His stomach called for more. He heard it shout. But he was a long time sending much more down, and still held nearly all the piece in his hand when the young eagles had finished all the rest. They gathered round, ready to snatch the meat away if they could. One of them pecked up the tooth that had come out, a little white speck with no roots. Antar felt that he had lost the only thing he knew among all that was round him now.

He was rescued by the sentinel, who came into the nest again, and moved him away to the edge, and watched over him while he continued his meal. He was obviously amazed at the way Antar managed. Antar was amazed too. After a long time he had eaten all he could. He went off to get a drink of water.

The day before the water had come straight from the melting snow of the mountain above. Its drops had fallen on him nearly as hard as ice, heavy with cold, and it had run clear and bright, the freshest water in the world.

Now Antar came to the little tumbling fall, where it scattered from a projecting rock, and found steam rising from it. The water was warm, but not the clean warm of a kettle. The steam had a smoky smell, as if kettle water had fallen on the coal fire.

The water itself was running rusty and staining the rock with red and green. It was warm to the touch, and Antar hung his hands in it and felt the warmth flow into his arms and right across him, comfortably.

He thought no one had ever done this before. There were no hot taps in his country because no one had thought of them. He filled the warm hands with water and drank some of it.

He spat it out at once. It tasted of old cinders and hot

brass, and stung his throat. He did not know how far down his throat it had gone, and he spat it out and spat it out, but could not get rid of the taste. He was still thirsty, and had to wash the taste away. Not far along the cliff were places where more water ran down, without steam.

The sentinel that had followed him stood on a rock not far away, watching. When Antar began to walk along the foot of the cliff to find another stream it hoppingly flew round and stood in front of him, barring his way.

"I am going to get a drink," said Antar. The bird did not understand, so Antar had to act out what he meant, waving his hands, pointing with his fingers, spitting and making faces and rubbing his throat to show what the water had done to him.

The eagle had difficulty understanding arms that were not wings. It seemed amazed when Antar cupped his hands together. It looked offended and pained when Antar told it loudly for the second time about the bad taste of the water. But at last it went to look for itself, because it was trying to understand.

It touched with its beak, and perhaps tasted. It shook its head and came walking clumsily back to Antar. It told him something, but Antar had no idea what it was. He went to find something to drink, so thirsty with bad tastes, dry throat, and spitting, that he pushed the eagle aside.

It immediately shrieked at him, flapped its wings, and pecked at his shoulder, but managed to turn the peck away at the last second, just when Antar was sure he would lose an arm. This was the beak that tore up an antelope to give him breakfast.

The eagle spread its wings, bowed its head, and stood before him ashamed, with eyes closed. It was meant not to hurt him. Antar knew that it had merely treated him like another eagle. Now it cowered before him as if he were the king.

It was sad for Antar to see the huge bird, as tall as he was even when its neck was bent down, apologizing. Antar reached up his hand and stroked the neck, smoothing the bronze feathers and running his fingers under them.

The bird opened its eyes, then closed them, then blinked with its inner eyelids, pleased at being scratched, and happy at being forgiven.

Antar felt better at not being pecked to death. He felt nearly happy at finding friendliness.

The eagle began to speak to him with the small sounds that eagles use among themselves, like the grating and grinding of gravel in a bucket, coming from the throat, not the beak.

Together they walked to the next tumble of water. Together they stood by it and discussed it. Neither of them knew what the other said, but they agreed, even if they did not know what that was either.

Antar wanted to dip a finger in the water, but the bird pushed his hand aside and was about to taste first. Antar pushed the beak aside. But nobody was getting a drink at all, this way. They managed, at last, to taste the water together, and found it had come pure down the cliff, cold from the snow.

They both drank. Then the eagle showed that it was still in charge. It gathered fallen rocks and stones and built up a little ridge just beyond the stream. Antar thought it was building a nest, or constructing a dam. But it was making a mark to show that he must not go further. When he put his foot over the little ridge, which was only a bump on the ground, the eagle pulled him back. With its grating voice it told him several things.

Antar understood, after a time, that *geeu* was water,

and that other sounds were for can and can't. He said his own name many times, "Antar, Antar, Antar," until all its meaning turned to echoes among the hills. The eagle repeated, "Gadar, Gadar, Gadar," which was as near as its speech could come. And Antar could say, "Garak, Garak," which was the eagle's name. The eagle words were hard, like finding out the words of a tune, and tunes are not words at all.

Before they went back to the nest Antar took the bird's beak in his hands and looked into its eyes, and at the bronze and black patterns at the base of the beak, telling himself that this was Garak, this design, this thing almost a word. Perhaps it was a word, but Antar had not yet learned to read anything.

During the day the mountains shook again. A dark cloud rose and blocked the sun, and ashes dropped from the sky. The grown eagles circled above the nest, father, mother, and Garak the sentinel, watching both above and below.

Further along the cliff, rocks rattled and roared down. A huge slide of snow buffeted and spluttered its way between spurs of the range, and there was lightning on the peaks and thunder in the valleys.

The flying birds knew there was peace before Antar did. They had been raised here and lived here, and knew the weather of the sky, the weather of the land, and the weather underneath it. They went hunting again.

Garak flew away, and another bird came in his place. Antar went to speak to it, but this bird was less easy to get on with, turning its head away from Antar, and looking as if he did not like him.

When the father eagle brought back a pheasant Antar was given no help by him, or by the new sentinel, and none at all by the young eagles. But they had always wanted to eat Antar, so he was not surprised, only hun-

49

gry. What he really wanted was some bread and butter and a boiled egg. But he could see that talking about boiled eggs might upset birds, even if he knew how to say it.

When night came he was once again tucked under the mother eagle, and made to go to sleep. The young eagles pecked and pestered him, pushing him out, wanting the warmest places for themselves.

In the night the mother eagle woke suddenly, trampling on him hard as she lifted herself into the air. Antar woke as well, and saw her flying up into the dark night.

There was a noise like buildings falling down and guns firing. It was not a dream. All round the nest, and on to it, were falling sticky lumps of burning rock, red-hot and smoking. The stuff of the nest, twigs and branches and weavings of grass and reeds, was taking fire. Flames were climbing in and out of it. Antar and the young eagles were ringed with fire, and would be roasted to death.

8

Antar jumped up, looking round for someone to help him. Hot air and cold air rushed past him in streaks that he could almost see. The young eagles ran about like ugly toys, flapping their stumpy wings, squawking, knocking each other over, and jumping into the air without being able to take flight.

No one came to help. There was no one but Antar in the high mountains, and he was alone with the eagles and the flames. It took him only a few small steps to leave the nest and stand beside the cliff. Now he had rock under his feet, not the firewood of the nest. But the young eagles would not leave, and the flames were eating into the nest in four or five places.

No more burning lumps were falling on the nest. Here and there, in the darkness, wandering stars of fire moved, where other fires fell on the bare flank of the mountain.

One of the burning places went out by itself. Antar ran forward and stamped on another, and that went out too. But one edge of the structure had two fires on it, and they joined to become one, sending up a sheet of flame too large to stamp on, or get near at all. Two more burning patches were bigger than could be stamped on.

At the foot of the cliff, near where the streams of water ran down, there were patches of snow, soft with spring weather but not yet melted. Antar ran and gathered a big snowball, carried it back, and dropped it into one of the smaller fires.

It made a black patch, and part of the fire was put out. Antar ran for more snow and made the patch larger. After seven snowballs that fire had gone out, and only steam rose from a hole in the nest. Now there was one big fire and one small one.

The nest had always smelled bad. The fire smoke was chokingly foul, and the steam sickening. Antar ran back for more snow.

"Just come and help," he shouted up to the dim shapes of circling eagles. "Come and get snow. Garak, come and get snow."

A moment later there was a dark shape on the ground beside him—Garak, hating the fire, but understanding what Antar meant; or wanting to understand, at least. He accompanied Antar to the heaps of snow, and stood helplessly by, not knowing what to do next.

"Feed the fire," said Antar, knowing that snow was a poisonous food for flames. Garak perhaps did not know what he meant, but could tell that Antar knew what he was doing.

"Take this," said Antar, rolling up snow and holding it up. Garak looked at it, working things out. Eagles do not think in the same way as people do, so Antar never knew what he thought. But Garak extended his wings, lifted himself with a few sweeps into the air, hung above Antar for a moment, and delicately took the snowball with his talons from Antar's hands.

He called out as he flew towards the fire. Before he

was at the nest another eagle hung over Antar, waiting for something to carry. Behind that one was another, and then one more winging in.

Garak dropped his ball of snow into the smaller fire, and swung away, coming back to wait in the line.

Antar packed up lumps of snow and held them up. His hands at first were stung with cold, and then warmed. Eagle after eagle came and took its burden from him and dropped it upon the nest.

Antar stopped after a time, when the snow below became too hard to dig with fingers. He went back towards the nest for a stick to scrape with.

There was still a crown of flames at one edge, and the nest seemed smaller. The little fires were out. The young eagles had stopped their panic, and were pecking at lumps of snow that had landed on the nest but missed the fire. There were enough lumps for Antar to gather together and throw into the large fire.

It seemed, though, that this fire was going to work its way through from underneath, throwing its heat ahead of itself and advancing without delay. It became too hot for the young eagles to stand. They did not have the sense to move away, but lay down where they were, gaping and breathing fast.

Antar threw snow, sweated with heat himself, and pushed a young bird away. None of them wanted to move, and preferred to come back into a huddle with the others. But he shifted them, and was greatly pecked for his trouble.

He had to sit down himself, worn out with heat and work his hands blistered with frost and fire, and a huge emptiness inside him. He was not hungry, but starved.

He sat in a sort of heat-faint, with his head spinning. He knew it was his head, not the nest or the mountains. While he sucked his fingers he felt the nest was in fact

53

shaking under him. There was a sudden upsurge of flame, and a huge heat washed over him, making his skin dry on his face.

There was a deep rumbling round him and under him. The fabric of the nest quivered and seemed to tip a little. The eagles on the wing above swirled away as flames, smoke, and sparks hurtled up towards them.

The nest vibrated now, and Antar had to hold on. At once something changed, and the world went dark. The fire at the edge of the nest had undermined itself and fallen off. Antar scrambled up and looked over the edge.

Below, falling in a flaring bundle, was the broken-off section of nest, falling down the ten-thousand-foot cliff, not mere flame, not red hot, but white hot with speed, and suddenly vanishing to nothing as it burnt out and exploded into ash. The ashes themselves did not touch the ground, but came floating up on the rising current of air.

Antar saw them swirl up, because the morning had returned, and light was in the sky.

The fire on the nest was not quite out, but it no longer roared. There were small flames, and nestlings of hot embers here and there along the edge.

Antar missed the heat, now that the dawn was cold. He was human and he missed fire. He set about killing the rest of it off because it was burning down the only home he had.

He thought that he should not kill it all. Maray and Aldect did not let him touch fire, but now he was in another place, and sitting on a huge mound of stuff that would burn. Nearby there was bare rock that would not burn. He could safely build a fire on that.

With great care and patience he lit more sticks pulled from the nest, and took fire away. He made a hearth at the foot of the cliff, and set fire in it, just as it lay at home under the chimney. There was no chimney here but the open air. Fire did not mind.

When his own fireside was burning he put out the remainder of the fire on the nest with snow, or by kicking it over the edge. He gathered the sticks from there and laid them ready to use by his own hearth, to burn as the day grew brighter.

The parent eagles came down to the nest, paced about on it, hating the smell of fire. They called to Antar twice, when they detected smoke. He had to dig his way in and put out a fire below on each occasion.

The first meal of the day came down on the talons of the father eagle. The young eagles became extremely excited, as usual. But Antar pushed in amongst them to get what he could of a long fish still twitching. Sharp beaks broke the fish up, and he took pieces away. He remembered what fire was for.

It is not easy to cook fragments of fish on a wood fire with no kitchen utensils at all. But it is possible, if you are prepared to eat ash.

The cooked fish smelt perfect, somewhere between burnt and raw, and was the best thing Antar had ever had, he was sure.

Later on he got the back half of a rabbit, burying it in ashes, then pulling tender meat from inside a charred skin. For a time he felt nearly happy.

Garak came down to him just as Antar wanted to sleep. Garak would not let him. When Antar's eyes closed for longer than a blink Garak's beak tapped him on the head.

"Go away," Antar shouted at last. "I don't want to talk to you."

But Garak was the best teacher. The other sentinels seemed not to like him, and would give him a peck if he did not understand at once. Only with Garak could

Antar peck back, and sometimes seem to share a joke. When Garak trod up and down, clenching and unclenching his talons, Antar was sure that was laughter. He grew to welcome Garak, who taught him more things than the other three could.

Day and night now he kept the fire going, sleeping by it in a pile of firewood from the nest. It was his kitchen and his living room, and his schoolroom when he could get Garak near the flames. The other three would not approach; though once or twice, when the fire was low, one of them had tweaked the heap of firewood to make it a better nest. But that was out of habit, not from a wish to be helpful.

The young eagles were getting bigger. They overtopped Antar, their wings grew long and feathers appeared through their down. They became extremely fierce, and their beaks were powerful. There were days when Antar could not get any food at all.

By this time, though, Garak and the others had taught him so many eagle words that he could ask for things. He knew more than the young eagles, but they would not give anything up. He asked Garak, and Garak had a fierce fighting argument with the parent eagles. After that he was brought food for himself at least once a day, but not absolutely every day.

One day, when Garak was not on duty, and Antar sat hungry but not cold, having had nothing for two nights, the mother eagle came down with something for him.

It was nothing large. She set it down at the edge of the nest, looked round at the sentinels, because they had to see that Antar ate, and were holding the young eagles back.

The food was not dead. It got up and walked about, looking for a friend. The young eagles rushed past their mother, wanting to catch and eat.

The food stuck its tail in the air, knowing that friends understood that, and meowed. It was a hand-sized fluffy kitten, grey, with blue eyes. It did not understand about being eaten. It was generally on the other end of the business.

Antar understood about being eaten. He had been brought a kitten to eat. He could not kill it and eat it, and only thought of rescuing it. He did that, banging a lot of eagle heads together, pushing the kitten inside his shirt, going back to his fire.

The kitten purred at him, then kneaded away at his chest with tiny claws. It crawled out, tried the ground, yawned at the fire, climbed up Antar's leg, and went to sleep on his lap.

Antar found that tears were coming from his eyes. He could not tell whether he was sad or happy, but he knew he was no longer alone. Also he had something to look after, which made him very bold. In a little while the father eagle brought a lamb to the nest. Antar put the kitten down, went to the nest, and took the whole lamb.

That evening he and the kitten roasted it completely, and sat side by side eating it, waking often in the night to have some more, until the kitten rolled on its back and showed its round belly. At dawn Antar felt that they could live like this, he and the kitten.

Later on, though, Garak came. He was not quite so pleased, Antar found. He did not mind the kitten, though he was tempted to swallow it without thinking because it was naturally appetizing.

He told Antar that he had not to eat much. He had to have only enough to keep himself alive. When Antar wanted to know why Garak could not yet explain. There was more to understand, he said, saying that when Antar was ready his lessons then would tell him.

The next day the other sentinels brought him bundles

of feathers, fallen from other eagles at moulting times. "Look at the young eagles," they said, "and see how they are fledging."

Antar saw the wing feathers growing strongly on the wings of the nestlings, and saw how they strove to fly.

"Grow these feathers," said the sentinels. "Grow wings."

Antar had to do what they said. He could not grow wings, but he could make them. He stuck them through the cloth of his coat, instructed by the sentinels, who showed him their wings and how the feathers lay and lapped one another. They pierced the holes for him, they combed the plumes straight. Antar had to find thorn and splinter to lock the shafts of the feathers into the cloth. Each feather not firmly fixed was pulled out, and had to be set in again.

By the end of the work he was sewing them in place with thread from his shirt, using a piece of bone to make a hole, threading through and pulling tight.

When he had made the wings he had to make the tail on the back of the coat; but there was no way of making it stretch and turn like that of an eagle.

Then, one day, Garak took him to the nest and stood him with the young eagles, inspecting them all. Antar found he was not so far off from them in tightness and trim. The kitten walked on his shoulder. They all eyed it, but did not try to eat it.

Garak left the nest when the mother eagle flew back. She had brought no food on this flight. She had other things in mind.

She went to the first of the young ones, pushed him from behind, and sent him over the edge of the nest, down the great drop, and he disappeared.

She treated the second in the same way. It fluttered on

the edge until she nipped its heels. The third followed, and then the small one, Keek.

Now there was only Antar left. He was thinking that now he would get a better share of the food, no matter what Garak thought. The mother eagle thought something different. She got behind Antar as if he were a young eagle, worked him to the edge so that he saw the depth below, and the clouds lying level halfway down.

"No," said Antar, clinging to the rough boughs of the nest, holding the kitten. "It's not me. I'm not . . ."

But she thought he was, and pulled away the wood he was holding on to, so that he began to tumble down the ten thousand feet of precipice, at the foot of which there was only the bottom of hard rock.

9

"What have we done?" said Antar, falling and spinning. The kitten clung to his shirt, began to crawl inside, and started to purr.

Antar stretched out his arms to hold on to something —a cloud, perhaps. But there was only air. Something else was falling with him, clutching and struggling just as he was. He had caught up with Keek. Keek was putting out his wings, and somersaulting down beside Antar.

Alongside there appeared Garak, falling in a swift dive.

"Fly," said Garak. "Gadar fly. Keek fly." Then Garak opened his own wings and stopped falling. Antar saw him grow small with distance, higher in the sky.

Antar turned in the air without being able to help it. Now he fell head first. He stretched out his arms, thinking of wings, knowing he had none. But something came up under him and held him steady, so that he no longer dropped and dropped. He was hanging on air, not falling through emptiness, supported by the feathers he had sewn on.

Beside him Keek had found the same thing. Then

Garak flew down in a great sweep and was the other side of him.

"Follow me," said Garak. He tipped himself to one side and swung away from the precipice. Inside Antar's shirt the kitten stopped clinging with claws and went to sleep.

Further along the cliff other young eagles were holding their places in the air, their parents beside them instructing them.

Garak lifted himself away with his wings. Antar tried to do the same thing, but did not have the power. He stayed where he was while Garak went into another circuit. Garak waited on a spiral, came round again and hung beside him.

Garak said some eagle words that meant they would try another way. He was disappointed, Antar could tell. The sounds he had used were those for disapproval, or for noticing strange things like the way Antar cooked his food or kept a kitten without devouring it in the night.

The other young eagles were rising higher again, not using their wings much. One of the sentinels cried out that Antar was flying like a dead bird.

Antar was thinking that he could fly home, that he would not mind the trouble he would get into for ruining his clothes.

"Follow again," said Garak. "We must get up to the nest again."

"Or my fire will be out," said Antar, deciding that the nest was his home at the moment, and that his arms were tired already.

Garak led him round on the level, then made him dive towards the cliff. Antar found that when he did so the air suddenly began to rush furiously past his face, then catch his wings, and then he was rising slowly.

But he did not have enough skill to stay on the air.

Nothing he and Garak could do between them hoisted him up. Keek found how to manage, and rose up and up. The other young eagles seemed lighter than air, and were at length no longer in the sky.

Only Antar and Garak were dropping slowly.

There were ledges and pinnacles here and there on the mountainside. Down at this level, just above the clouds, the steepness was not so great. Garak alighted on a sharp ridge, and Antar beside him. Antar's landing was more like hitting the ground. He rolled and slid, then clung and climbed beside Garak. The kitten made an indignant noise at being squashed in the process.

"You have eaten too much," said Garak. "You are too heavy. A whole lamb cannot fly. We should eat the food you are carrying."

"I am not strong, either," said Antar. But for the moment the only thing he could do was take off his boots, and put them tidily and safely beside a rock. He removed his stockings too, and folded them up inside the boots.

"We have heard how humans moult in the night and grow a new plumage," said Garak. "Now I have seen it. You have another hand on each leg. Have they been there all the time?"

Antar looked at his toes. "They will not hold anything," he said. Garak looked at his own talons, then gave his strange sort of laugh, clenching and unclenching them and blinking. He leaned down and lifted each boot in turn.

"That is a great weight lost," he said. "We shall try again."

It is one thing to be pushed off the cliff by a caring mother eagle. You are over and down before thinking about it. If you do it yourself you think first, and you know it can't be done.

Antar did it when Garak pecked his heels. At once

Antar had his wings working, very cross, with tears of fright and hurt falling from his face, and ready to hit his friend.

Flying was easier now. He was a long way from Garak's standard, and could not tell what to do with his legs. He thought he might be better without them while he was in the air. Garak managed to get him to swing up as he left the face of the cliff, so that when he dived back into the rising air he did not drop lower. Then, when he was in the rising current he flew level and that raised him yet again.

The circuits grew more and more wing-wearying, but after nine or ten of them the clouds were specks far below, and the nest, with its black, burnt sides, was at the same level. Then, with an effort, Antar tumbled to the ground.

His landing was better than the last one, but the ground was so uncomfortable to his bare feet that he stumbled and fell.

He put his wings by and ran to the fire. It was still alight. He built it up again, had a drink of water, and sat down.

Garak came back, did a funny landing like Antar's, and sat close by.

"Now you begin to learn and understand," he said. Standing there erect and solemn he continued to teach Antar.

There were so many things to know, he found. These eagles on these mountains were the greatest in the world. They knew things that other birds did merely by instinct. They knew why they did things.

"It is like people," said Antar. "But we do not always know."

Garak continued his teaching. Antar, weary with his

first flying, cold without boots and socks, hungry without a meal, heaped wood on the fire and went to sleep.

While he slept Garak went away, and Antar was sorry to have been so impolite. He was also sorry when the other sentinels now came to teach him.

He had two more flights that day, one over the precipice again, and one over the mountain slope beside the nest. The sentinels taught him without much patience. They did not let him near the young eagles any more, so he got no more food there. They brought him what he was allowed, and it was not much.

"You will be too heavy for us," they said. He understood from what they told him that they needed a child to do something for them involving flying. The child had to be brave and not afraid of heights, wiry and small, and old enough to be sensible.

If he could not be these things he would be left to fend for himself in the snows, because he would be useless to the eagles, and too much trouble to return to his home.

They taught him how to behave among eagles. He had to understand which eagles were above him in importance and wisdom, and treat them with respect. He had to learn how to treat those below him in importance and age: that is, eagle age, not human age.

He had to know what food an eagle may eat, and what time of year. During their flights he was shown where different sorts of food had its home, whether it lived in tree-tops, holes in the rocks, or burrows in the sands, or in shallow water. There is no food among houses, he was taught. Men are there, and traps, and guns.

"I know," said Antar, remembering a drop of blood on his hand.

"That was our Great Eagle," said the sentinel teaching him. "He has not recovered from his wound and is hardly able to fly. Men are our enemy, and you are our slave, Gadar." They all called him Gadar now. It meant Goose in eagle language, which seemed right to the eagles though it was an accident of sound.

He learnt how to distinguish wing signals from other birds, which was a separate language of its own. He could hardly speak it with his wings because they were so stiff and clumsy. When it came to language of the tail feathers, and their use, he was dumb and useless.

But he thought about things, because he was being pecked and hit by three of the sentinels for flying badly and not giving messages with tail and wing. When Garak came back he was not only glad to see him as a friend, but was able to fly with him down the cliff to find his boots again. All he wanted was the stockings. He came back with them to the fireside. While Garak taught him claw signs, which his toes could not do, and eye signs, which he was very good at with his big human eyes, he stitched feathers to the stockings, and made himself a feathery tail useful for flying.

It made so much difference to him that he could outfly Garak and turn more quickly. Also he could crash more easily, which was painful.

"Eggs are not hatched in a day," said Garak.

"But knees are broken," said Antar, sorry for himself once on a remote peak, putting snow on scratches.

"While you are sitting there I shall tell you how to see the wind," said Garak. "You see more than we do, but less sharp. All the same, you will have to know."

There were lessons and rules, about staying dry, about staying out of trees, about avoiding smoke, because men are in smoke, as are other things no eagle understood.

He learnt too that in winter, or in droughts, eagles must not be too particular about what they eat. They do not have to kill, but may eat things found dead, things they could never kill, like oxen or horses or lions. He was taught the tender parts of those animals, and decided not to eat stomach even if he had to.

He was taught that even eagles may be eaten when found dead in hard times, because all eagles together are more important than one eagle. But that if he had to do such a thing he must bring back the feathers of the left wing, so that history could remember.

He was taught, most of all, that he must obey the Great Eagle, the bird that had taken him from the church tower. The Great Eagle's spies had chosen him, and waited for the right time.

"They chose me?" said Antar. "What for?" He knew there was a reason, and that he had not been told it.

"You are the one," said Garak. "You will be remembered in all our history."

"Why?" asked Antar.

But Garak would not say.

Antar went on being taught, learning, flying, catching at last some of his own food; being scolded for eating a delicious meal of berries, sweet and juicy; mastering the sky; gradually being able to begin a flight without jumping off a high cliff, only needing a run and a small slope to become airborne.

One day, all four sentinels came for him.

"Set your feathers in order," they said, grooming him with their own beaks, because he had always found that difficult. "The Great Eagle has sent for you. He will tell you why you are here and what you are to do."

10

The Great Eagle lived on a pinnacle of the mountains that was too high for Antar to reach by flying. The sentinels led him up as high as he could go, in and out of rising currents, along the invisible rivers that flow up the mountains. These rivers of the air can sometimes be seen by watching the clouds form on mountain tops. At other times only the wing-tips of an eagle can discover them.

Eagles fly with their fingers, Antar found. He flew with the thickness of his arms, because his fingers were too short to have strength. An eagle's fingers are sensitive, like a man's, and feel the way along the living airs.

Perhaps Antar was too heavy, and the wrong shape. But time after time, as they circled the pinnacle, the sentinels were lifted above him, and he could not find the next step in the spiral of the sky.

He was able to see that there was no way of climbing the pinnacle. Its sides went up a hundred feet as straight as the sides of a box, with no ledge or holding place at all, and then there was an overhang of nest material. On the nest stood the Great Eagle himself, his head turning while he watched Antar.

"You cannot get there," said Garak at last.

"I can hardly breathe," said Antar, because the air was dry, cold, and thin, and rough in his throat.

Another sentinel flew to the Great Eagle, hung in the air beside the nest, and talked with him. Garak led Antar away.

They stayed as high as they were, but the ground rose to meet them when they approached the flank of the mountain. The mountain went up into the highest clouds, and its top was never clear, Garak said. Only one thing lived there, but Garak would not say what it was. "I do not know," he said.

Antar landed against a slope like the side of a steeple, clutching at snow, scraping at ice, and holding at last. He realized that he was not afraid, that if he fell he could fly away. For the moment his arms rested, carrying only half his weight.

Garak made him use his legs. "You must climb higher," he said. "You will fly from the height and glide down to the Great Eagle's pinnacle. There is no other way for you to get there."

Antar climbed. He was left alone by Garak, who flew back to the pinnacle, and then to the mountain, to judge the height and test the air. He waited for Antar at a great height, above a tremendous cliff of ice.

Antar climbed in a wilderness of rock and snow, ice and cold winds. Garak called to him; the other sentinels watched and flew in the air beside him. Once, when he rested after a particularly hard climb, they came and pecked at his ankles as they had before. They did not let him pause.

Garak did not let him stop either. As soon as Antar was beside him he made him look at the place he must fly to. They were high above the pinnacle now, and it did not show very distinctly against the background of rock and patchy snow.

"He is ready," said Garak, meaning that the Great Eagle was prepared. But Antar had not even found the nest. Eagles have sight that pulls things closer. "Fly now, Gadar."

Antar flew, plunging from the ice cliff, finding the air too weak to hold him, but spreading his wings and his tail feathers and holding himself up with his mind.

"Fly, fly," said Garak. "Wings, wings."

Antar flew; but wing-beats did not keep him up, and he still seemed to sink as he went, wing-tip to wing-tip with Garak and another sentinel, a third leading, and the fourth trailing.

"Now soar," Garak called. "Gather speed, Gadar."

"Gadar, Gadar," called the others, jeering at him, meaning he was a goose.

The pinnacle had separated from the background now, but it was rising still into the sky, because Antar was below it. He did not see that he had done anything useful by climbing the mountain for more than an hour. Then he could not see at all, because the rushing air filled his eyes with tears and the tears broke into ice and made him blind.

"Now lift with tail feathers, and fly, Gadar," said Garak. And all at once, with a lifting wind under him, with his speed, the pinnacle seemed to tip and sink. "Drop," said Garak.

Antar dropped, closed his wings, and was tumbling on the nest of the Great Eagle. The Great Eagle was stepping to one side (like Garak understanding a joke, but the Great Eagle was not amused at all) to avoid the rolling figure.

Antar stood up, dizzy with what he had done. The four sentinels stood calm as statues on the edge of the nest. Antar looked at his rumpled feathers, rubbed his knees, which now were completely through the new trousers, and looked up at the Great Eagle.

"I cannot eat that," said the Great Eagle, clearly and slowly, looking down at Antar.

"He means he cannot understand you," said Garak, quickly, just as Antar began to feel alarm creeping all over him. "He does not think you will be useful."

Antar felt he was not useful. He was out of breath, untidy, and had not got here under his own power. The sentinels came forward, and with heads bowed at the presence of the Great Eagle, tidied Antar up, grooming him hard for the second time that day, and stood him up again.

"I think I shall go home," said Antar, because he did not like being ordered about by a lot of birds, even if they were his own size.

"No," said Garak. "You must now listen. The Great Eagle has something to ask you. Then you may go home, if the other eagles will let you."

"I shall speak, Garak," said the Great Eagle. But for a long time he was silent. He turned his head with the huge beak to one side and touched a place below his left wing. There were broken feathers, and blood ran out of a wound where the bullet had entered. The Great Eagle's left wing dropped with pain and weakness, and he could not stay upright. He crouched down as if he were roosting for the night on a clutch of eggs. The sentinels crouched down in the same way, so that they were not above their leader.

"Go down too, Gadar," said Garak. "He is the highest of us."

"I am a man," said Antar. "I shall sit, because I am a tired man, not because I am less than any eagle."

"You are a man," said the Great Eagle. "I am a

70

wounded one of my kind. Many years ago, before I came from the egg—and I am the eldest of all living eagles—men and eagles lived without quarrelling. That was in the golden times of the world. But things have changed. Men have made fields where there were forests, and pastures on the sides of the mountain, and over the years the lands the eagles watched have grown less and less. Eagles died because they could not find food; men shot eagles for taking animals they had brought. The eagles were driven away from all the lands of men, up into the mountains only."

The Great Eagle paused, raised himself up, and looked round at the mountains he was talking about. "Then men came into the mountains too. They came for lead and copper, gold and silver, which were underground. Eagles had begun to fear them, which was not as it had been when Eagles stood among men as equals and talked in the councils. Now men would kill eagles and take the feathers for decoration. But they did worse than that."

He lowered himself again, and looked upon his wound. "This harm they have done me is bad, but I forgive them. They no longer know what is good and right. I was flying where men watch the ground, and I was carrying away one of their young ones. I was not taking him to young eagles for them to eat his bones. I wished to eat his sense for myself, so that he can do a thing for eagles. But I cannot make him. Garak, have you told him what he is here for?"

"No, Sire," said Garak. "We have made him as close as we can to one of ourselves. He can fly, but in fact he knows little about that, and nothing about the reason. I have grown to like him, though he has been young a long time."

"I have been old a long time," said the Great Eagle. "Longer than men live have I been the Great Eagle. Lis-

71

ten, Gadar. Once or twice in a hundred years one of our kind lays the egg that will be the next Great Eagle. When that egg is laid we know it for what it is, because of certain signs. It is taken away from the nest it belongs to, and is kept safely in a certain place. When the living Great Eagle is dying, as I am dying now from old age and my wound, that egg is to be hatched. Have you understood me, Gadar?"

"I have understood," said Antar. "Is the young eagle from that egg to eat me first of all its food?"

"No, indeed," said the Great Eagle. "You are to be honoured and given a long life."

"Or a short one," said one of the sentinels to another, and laughing like Garak with his feet, slyly.

"That will depend on your skill and sense," said the Great Eagle. "We wish you a long life, but may give you a short one. We cannot tell."

"I'd like to go home, best of all," said Antar. "When I can."

"That is where you shall be," said the Great Eagle. Then he paused again and closed his eyes in pain and sickness.

Antar did not know what was to come next. He was wondering whether he was the egg that was being talked about; or whether he was to change homes and be the next Great Eagle; or indeed whether he had himself hatched from the egg.

The Great Eagle opened his eyes and spoke again. "The egg is to be hatched," he said. "It is known from being the colour of the cold sun. Men, looking for gold, found the safe place in the mountains. Gold is the cold stuff of the sun, and men took away the egg that is the next Great Eagle. We know where it went, but we have been unable to recover it. Tell him more, Garak. I am too weary now."

The Great Eagle was now a bundle of feathers, like a dead thing. Three sentinels spoke to one another, and moved to look after him. All they could do was guard him, standing at either side and at his head, watching outwards.

Garak continued, "The egg was taken down the mountain and sold to a king. We do not understand selling, but the man who found the egg had four farms afterwards, many cattle, and a large number of sheep. However, he did not raise all his lambs. The egg went to one of the nesting grounds of men. They call it a town, and all the living places have a roof, like the nests of small birds. Under the hardest roof in town lies the egg, hidden in some place. It is part of the treasure of the king."

"Tell him of the battle," said the Great Eagle in a whisper.

"Once," said Garak, "when I was young and not allowed to go, the eagles went to the town and tried to recover the egg. Of all that went only one came back, with a broken wing. He walked all winter, eating mice and other small things, came to the territory of the eagles, and then died. He was my father, and I remember all he said. Before he died he told the tale of the battle, of eagles lifting the roofs of houses and searching within; of men coming out with guns and bows and spears; of men and eagles dying in the fight; of finding only the place where the egg was kept. In the centre of the king's nest there is a fire. At the end of the nest there is a nest with something in front of it so we could not get in. Inside that place, in another nest made for it, is the egg. Do you understand?"

Antar thought he understood that Garak was telling him of a hall with a fire in it, and a cupboard at one end holding the egg in a box or basket or thing an eagle could only call a "nest."

"I understand," he said.

"He has understood, Sire," said Garak.

"Then send him on his way," said the Great Eagle. "That is why he is here."

"The egg must be brought back," said Garak, "by a man; but only a child can be brought here and taught to fly. We have waited for the right child, and it is you, Gadar. We watched you, and we knew you were small enough, and wise enough to help us. Whether you are brave enough is something only you can know. But you understand that the egg must be found and brought here for hatching, or we shall be left without a Great Eagle and we shall all be no more."

All five eagles looked at Antar. The Great Eagle was measuring him with his eyes; Garak and the three other sentinels were insisting with their gazes.

Antar walked forward and squatted down in front of the Great Eagle. The three sentinels were ready to drive him away, but the Great Eagle murmured at them, and they drew back.

Antar knew what he must do. He knew that two eagle friends were better than three eagle enemies. He knew that the eagles had done their best for him, putting aside their fierce and greedy natures to be kind to him. They had not, for instance, eaten him or his kitten.

He lifted the tired head of the Great Eagle from the floor of the nest and placed it on his knees. It was huge, and very much alive in his hands. He smoothed the neck, running his fingers under the feathers. He looked into the eyes that had pleaded with him. As he scratched gently, just as he had scratched and pleased Garak, the eyes blinked and the beak opened a little, and the Great Eagle made the pleased sounds of a newly hatched chick.

Then he lifted his head, got to his feet, and with his own beak groomed the wings of Antar.

"I eat your understanding," he said.

Because Antar, unable to speak because he thought he might cry, had shown clearly that he would do what the eagles wanted him to do.

When he had done that all the sentinels came and bowed in front of him, to show that he was greater than they were. And then they took him away, back to his own nest and fireside.

11

There was no fireside when Antar came back to it. The shadows of night were creeping up the valleys, and there was darkness far below. There was no glow of spark, no welcoming whisper of flame, in his hearth. The kitten sat close under a warm stone, mewing desperately, frightened of all eagles, and hungry.

Garak landed beside Antar. The other sentinels went down to the nest where the four young ones and their parents were gathering for the night.

"They are coming to wish you a good watch, Gadar," said Garak.

"A good watch?" said Antar. He knew that watching was hunting, having territory of your own, and keeping yourself.

"Yes," said Garak. "You know where you are going."

"I do not know when," said Antar.

"Now," said Garak. "You fly by night. If you fly over the lands by day men will fire a gun at you." He actually said that men would "throw hot stone into you," but Antar understood clearly.

Antar did not think men would shoot a boy, even if he

was flying. Then he remembered that he was not going back to his own people, but far in the opposite direction. People there might do anything.

Nine eagles came up from the nest. The largest was the father, tall and dangerous. The smallest was Keek, now as big as Antar, with a beak covered in blood from his latest meal. He was as savage as any wild hunting bird. The sizes in between were the mother, the other young ones, and the sentinels.

"Also," said Garak, continuing the reasons for flying at night, "you are to fly towards a certain star, and we shall show it to you. That star will end the night over the town where you must find the thing you are searching for."

The eagles knew what Antar had not realized, that it is very difficult to explain to anyone exactly which star you want them to look at. Stars are very much alike, and look as if they have tumbled from a torn sack and been scattered everywhere.

Garak's method was simple. "Look," he said, and Antar looked. Of course he saw nothing but the glowing sand of all the galaxies and clusters. Garak could only tell him in which direction to look. Then he sent the other eagles up to hang on the air, one by one. He directed each one to an exact place, to the right or left, further away or closer, until he had them grouped as he wanted them.

By that time Antar had begun to see which star he was to follow, the bright one of a small cluster.

"I see it," he said.

"But you must be certain," said Garak. He called the eagles down, and they stood in a ring round Antar again. "Now which star is it?" Garak asked. "Can you tell, Gadar?"

"No," said Antar, because he had lost the tiny bead of

light in all the broken necklace of sky. "They are all the same again."

So the eagles flew up again, patiently. Antar could hear some small grumbles, particularly from the sentinels.

"I have been an eagle a short time," he said. "My eyes are still different. I am doing my best."

He did his best. After he had been shown three times he found the star easily. "I know it by heart," he said.

"Then go," said Garak. All the other eagles walked solemnly back to the nest, turning their backs on him. They settled down in the dusk if they were that family, or swung away to their own places if they were sentinels.

"I shall go a little way with you," said Garak. "Not far, and not out of my own watch."

"Now?" said Antar.

"Now," said Garak.

Antar looked at his dead fire. This was no longer home. He picked up the kitten and stowed it inside his shirt. It still said things about being hungry.

"That's right," said Garak, lifting into the air. "Take a snack with you."

Antar, weary from the day, full of hunger, cold, and very frightened, lifted himself from the edge of the nest and flew up slowly into the dark, to fly for an unknown long time and an unknown how far.

He located the star and turned towards it. Beside him Garak flew at Antar's speed. The last sunlight fell off the mountainsides, and there was only starlight.

Somewhere in that thin light Garak turned away with a last call of "Good watching," and Antar was alone.

He flew on towards the star. He was thinking that it guided him towards an unknown place. But if he turned round and flew towards another star he would find himself at home, by a real fireside, among people who loved him without wanting him to travel to unknown towns to rescue lost eggs.

He circled where he was, looking for a clue. What star would shine over his own town? What light would make the cross on the church shine?

He did not know that at that very moment of time a man from the country had come to his father's house door, carrying a thing made of cloth. He did not know that Aldect had called Maray to see the cloth; or that Maray and Roslin had taken it and known what it was.

"It came tumbling out of the sky," said the man. "They told me it might be news for you; but I did not expect it would be bad news."

He gave the cap that had fallen from Antar's head into their hands. "Some bird took it from somewhere," he said. "I reckon."

"It took the boy as well," said Aldect. "An eagle stole him."

So then the man left. Maray and Roslin set the cap on the table, and Aldect knew he could never make them content again.

Round Antar, circling beyond the mountains, there grew a lightness in the sky. The moon had come out from behind the rocks. He could see now for miles beyond him and below him. He heard, back at the mountains, the stirring of feathers and a call from an eagle throat, telling him to turn and fly on, not to loiter in the air. He had been seen dallying.

He found the star again. He stretched his wings once more, and flew steadily on, sure now that he had first to do what the eagles wanted. They had promised that he would return home at last; but they had not promised he would live long enough to do so. They did not know whether he would succeed.

He went on in the moonlight. Once a black bird came

up and looked in his eye before dropping down to distant forests of mighty trees deep in a valley below.

Once a patrol of high-flying bats came and circled his head. The kitten came out to hear what they broadcast to one another. They made a fresh formation and flew to examine other objects.

He saw a shooting star flying the far side of the sky, falling among the peaks of unknown mountains.

Down below there was a huge valley, and he was following the length of it as it curved gently across the land. In it there was a river, tumbling and gurgling as it ran from the mountains, then exploding over a great cataract, and after that flowing still and smooth. Beside it, down in the dark, Antar heard hunting owls call, wolves howl, bears snarl, and almost felt the running hooves of bison or wild horses on frozen ground.

The star he followed dipped towards the horizon, sinking lower with the night. Antar caught the smell of wood smoke once or twice from outlying camps, and saw fire below, brighter than the gleam of moon on river or lake.

He smelt the smell of men. That is made up of cows, sheep, fire, men themselves, horses and leather, open ground dug up to show the earth, and cooking food. There was too the strange smell of hot water in kitchens and workshops.

There was fire in plenty to be seen soon, and then the town itself. It lay close against the river, with wooden walls made from tree trunks standing upright. There were boats on the river, horses on the banks, and sentries watching land and water.

None of them watched the sky. None of them knew they were under the star Antar followed. They did not know that over their town it touched the ground.

When it did, Antar drew his wings in and approached

the earth, drawing them out again to cup the air and bring himself to a halt on the wooden wall itself.

He made a good landing for a flying boy. Garak would have laughed, or the other sentinels sneered.

Here the sentries were amazed and alarmed. Two of them ran away, and two of them ran forward. But they all started talking.

Antar jumped down to the ground, using his wings to steady himself. If he had not he would have broken a leg, at least, jumping house-high down. His landing this time was not quite perfect, and he rolled over. The kitten squeaked.

Two sentries came clambering down ladders and pointed spears at him. The two that ran away came back with friends. They surrounded Antar, talking and shouting.

After a little time Antar realized that he had forgotten how to talk. He could not understand a word. In fact he could not tell where any word began or ended. None of it meant anything to him. I only know eagle, he said to himself.

In fact, if he had been able to speak he would not have known what to say. Neither the Great Eagle, nor Garak, had given him any idea how to do what he had been sent to do. He knew that he could not ask for the egg, but that was all. Of course, now he had forgotten every word it did not matter. But he would have liked to hear something he knew.

He spoke to them in the eagle tongue. He said his name was Gadar. But they thought he had a sore throat.

The sentries stopped being frightened after a time, and started to finger his feathers. They began to understand that he was a boy, and began to tease him. Antar could tell they were laughing at him because he would get into trouble from his mother for coming out at night dressed like that.

One of them rumpled the hair on his head, in quite a kindly fashion. They sent for one of the women of the town.

Antar had almost forgotten such things. She took him by the hand and led him to a house. Antar went in with her, and felt very strange.

He had not been in a house for a long time.

He tried to sit on a chair, but his tail feathers would not let him. The woman looked at his hands. They looked right to Antar, but the woman thought they were dirty, and began to wash them. She wanted to pull away feathers that Antar had strapped to them, but he would not let her. She became angry. Antar could tell that she was saying things about only wanting to help him, and that he should be grateful.

The kitten meowed and looked out. Now, everyone understands kittens, which have no feathers, and spend a lot of time washing their hands and feet. The kitten got a dish of milk at once. Antar got his face rubbed with a wet cloth.

The woman said silly things to the kitten. She scolded Antar for being sulky. You don't always need words to understand what is being said. Then he was given a piece of bread, and ate it all at once. It was the best bread he had ever eaten. He was given a drink of something hot, and did not like the heat or the taste.

The drink had been heated on a fire. Antar went to squat in front of it, like an eagle, and then fell asleep on his feet. He had been awake all night, and his arms wanted to fall off. His muscles were stretching and slackening as if he still flew, and his head was heavy with want of sleep.

When he woke up he forgot for a moment where he

was and tried to fly out of the trap he was in. He went up to the roof of the house and came down again, flapping his wings and calling to Garak to help him.

Then he remembered he was a boy, not an eagle. He remembered that he had come here for a special eagle purpose, and that he was a spy, an enemy, and had to keep his wits about him.

When he settled down again, perched on a corner of the table, the woman came and spoke softly to him.

Antar remembered that not all men speak the same language. He had not forgotten how to speak, but he had forgotten there were other ways of doing it.

It was too late. Two men came into the room suddenly. They grabbed Antar, holding his arms close to him so that he could not fly, pulled him out of the house, and put him in a small cage, where he could not stretch his arms, or wings.

Then they picked up the cage and carried him away in it.

"Meow," said the kitten, who had gone to sleep inside his shirt again.

12

Antar had no chance to see where the cage was being taken. Before it had crossed the street outside, a man came running up with a blanket. Antar hoped he was to have it to sit on and wrap round himself, because he was cold and being bumped about.

The blanket was hung over the cage. Antar could see nothing. Nobody could see him. He thought he would drag an edge or corner inside, because he could reach it perfectly well, but it would not come. The blanket had been tied underneath very severely.

The cage went jogging along, men shouting to clear the way, others shouting back, the cage being jostled and tipped, jerked and swung. Antar felt dizzy and unwell in the dark place. It was smelly too, because the blanket was very old and unwashed.

There were holes in it, but they showed only dark or light, and swung about in front of his eyes until he felt sick.

Then he fell to one end of the cage. The men were now going up some stairs, he guessed, because the tip of the floor was steeper than any slope they could walk. He had ' to lie where he was, comforting an alarmed kitten, his head banged, and his wings crushed under him.

The cage levelled out, and there was darkness outside. No gleams of light came from the edge of the blanket or through its worn holes.

The cage was put down suddenly, and remained still. Antar's head went on swimming. The men walked away, the sound of their feet hollow on a wooden floor. A door swung hard into its frame, and closed solid.

There was darkness. There was absolute quiet. Nothing moved beyond the blanket, not a sound made itself heard.

Antar felt he was completely alone. Even the kitten seemed not to belong to him, or want to be with him. It opened its eyes wide.

If I can see that, thought Antar, then it isn't quite all darkness. There was a grey light filling the place where the cage was, and creeping unwillingly into the cage, unfriendly, not wanting to be useful.

The kitten crawled out between the bars, spending a long time looking down, then leaping out. It was strange, Antar thought, that he did not hear it land on the floor below. When he stretched down an arm after it he found it curled up in a sag of blanket, sleeping off its milk.

Antar thought he was in a room, or prison. He thought a prison was more likely. Two prisons, one a cage, the other a cell.

I am in the little one, the kitten is in the bigger one, he thought.

Outside the cage the room was empty. Only empty-room noises came from it, the click of wood talking to itself, the rattle of a window in a distant breeze, the quiet yawn of a roof stretching as it grew warmer or colder.

Antar began to straighten his wings. He could not stand up to do it, because the cage was not tall enough.

He had to kneel to preen his wing-feathers as he had been taught, but with his fingers, not a beak. He managed one wing, and half the other, and found he was kneeling there doing nothing.

He thought he had a dream of being at home before the fire, with Roslin prattling, Maray cooking, Aldect going off to work. It was so real that it was cruel to be woken from it. When he woke, cramped on his knees, his neck twisted, he found tears running down his face.

After a time he curled himself up without hurting his feathers and went to sleep. He pulled feathers back from his thumb and sucked it. He felt the cage and the room beyond it, the whole city and its strange-speaking people, go away. He was asleep.

He slept like a boy, not like an eagle. No eagle sleeps so soundly.

When he woke there was noise all round him. There was bright light coming into the cage. At first he did not know where he was, and hoped he had come home to his own bed and that his own town was moving outside, and the bells ringing, and that all he remembered between was a dream.

But, first, he had wings on him still. And next, he was in a strange place. Beyond the blanket there was light, the glittering flames of candles. There was noise, of men and women busy at something. There were the sounds of what they were doing, and the smells of it too. There was fire. They were cooking.

Spits were turning, fat was sizzling, puddings were boiling, basins were being stirred, bread was being kneaded, bones chopped, onions sliced, garlic crushed, herbs bruised. Apples were roasting, honey melting, butter churned, nuts cracked, custards poured, cheeses opened.

There was a huge smell of cooked food. There was

warm air coming into the cage. Antar felt that perhaps things might be all right for him very soon. He was glad they were getting him something to eat.

He started calling out that he was there, that he was ready, and could he please watch? His stomach shouted as well, and he heard it.

Someone looked in at him, round the edge of the blanket. That person called to others, and pulled the blanket away.

Antar was dazzled by the candles, by the fire, by the shining of silver bowls and beakers, by glistening knives and jars of rich wine.

The fire was in a huge hearth at the end of a room. The room itself was high, its long roof supported by wooden pillars painted gold. There was a wide table with benches, and the prepared food was being put on the table by cooks, servant girls, soldiers, and people that might be princes or butlers.

Soldiers, girls, and cooks came to look at Antar, and the princes, or butlers, came to tell them to get back to work. They looked at Antar instead.

One of them put in a short sword, not to hurt him but to make him move about, using it as a stick. He wanted Antar to spread his wings.

Antar looked at his wings, and he was ashamed. Garak would have been extremely angry to see feathers so untidy, and would have pecked him much worse than the man with the sword.

It was necessary, Garak said, to have wings in readiness at all times. At every moment they must be ready. And Antar's wings were ready for nothing. He began at once to make them straight again, to lay the feathers in their true overlaps, to set the strands together so that they would hold air.

All the people came to watch. Antar spread one wing,

then the other, but did not have enough room to do the work properly. He knew that was no excuse. He did not know what he would say if Garak came here now.

He took no notice of being prodded by swords or long spoons (which happened next). He went on with the things he had been trained to do. Wings came before food, and Garak had made that clear many times. If you had no wings you had no food. If you had food you settled your wings before eating it.

Antar's wings had always needed more care than true eagles' wings. They were artificial, and not so good in any case.

The soldiers soon had enough of watching. The butlers tired of it after a time. The cooks went back to their basting and proving. Only the servant girls watched longer.

Outside the room trumpets sounded. The room of people arranged itself in some way, a little like a wing being made ready for flight. The butlers stood in a row, the soldiers lined up along a wall, the cooks set their caps straight, the girls smoothed their aprons, and patted their hair flat on top and up at the sides.

The door opened. A gust of cold air walked into the room. Antar watched it slip along the floor to the fireplace, then curl up into the rafters. Being with the eagles had taught him to watch the moving of air.

After the night air came the king, to his supper. With him came his people. He looked first towards the table, then over towards Antar. He came across to Antar. He was just a little old hungry man, wearing golden things round his neck, and a gold thing like a belt round his head, walking with a stick that had a gold knob.

He studied Antar with wrinkled-up eyes. Then he gave some orders.

The first order was about opening the cage. The cage

was opened, and the soldiers drew their swords. Antar might be wholly dangerous, they thought.

Antar climbed out on to the floor. It would have been better if he had not trodden on the kitten, which was still asleep on a corner of the blanket. No one had seen it because it was the same grey colour.

The kitten screeched. Antar jumped, and the swords were against his chest. Antar bent and picked up the kitten. The king reached out his hand and took the kitten from him. Then he held it up and offered it to Antar's mouth, wanting him to eat it, to swallow it, there and then.

The kitten, however, scratched the king, spat at him, and walked round Antar's neck, because it was Antar's pet.

The king did not mind. The soldiers longed to run their swords through Antar, but he merely stood where he was, hoping to be invited to eat some of the food.

The king gave another order. When the order was carried out Antar remembered what the Great Eagle and Garak had told him he had come for. There was a nest, he had been told, and the king's treasure is in there. The egg is in another nest inside that nest. And here was the king, and perhaps this was the room.

The soldiers took a bar from the wall, and lifted part of the wall off. Behind that was a cupboard. Garak had called it a nest because eagles have no houses or furniture, only themselves and nests. Inside that cupboard was the treasure.

Not all of it was wanted now. Antar had been recognized as an eagle and belonging to the king. The king had other eagle things, and he had them brought out now. Antar watched, with eagle eyes, or as much like them as he could.

First there came a bundle of feathers. They were

strung on a cord, and the soldiers hung them up like decorations along the wall. They were old and dusty, and moths had eaten them.

Next there was an eagle on a post, long dead, stuffed, and standing uncomfortably. It too was turning grey with age and decay. It had glass eyes that saw nothing. Antar saw the patterns on its beak, and knew it had been related to Garak. Now it stood all on one side in the candlelight and firelight, and filled the room with sadness.

The eagle was stood at one end of the table, lonely and far from its mountains. It was treated with respect, Antar thought. It was thought an honourable thing. More sad were the next things to be brought out. There were eight skulls of eagles, each one mounted on a slice of wood, with a few bones of the neck there too. Once there had been feathers and skin, but on most of them it had fallen away, and the white bone showed.

They had been neglected, and from the eye socket of one of them a mouse fled across the table, jumping desperately down from the far end, and vanishing into the shadows.

Antar found himself being held back, because his eagle instincts or teaching had made him lift with his wings and chase.

Next there was a set of curious stones of many colours, brought out and dusted. They were from the mountains, Antar thought. But they were not what he hoped to see. He knew there was a nest inside the nest of the cupboard, and that the thing he was seeking lay there.

A basket was brought to the table. Something was in it, folded in a cloth. The king himself went forward to unwrap it. Antar felt that here was the thing he had come for, and wanted to look too, to be sure.

He did not know what he could do if he saw it. He was

helpless among all these people, with swords and spoons and shut doors. And, really, he wanted something to eat much more than he wanted almost anything.

The wrapped thing was uncovered, carefully, and laid on a dish at the end of the table. The king called for more light, and candlesticks were brought.

The king smoothed the thing with his own hand, and the candlelight glittered on it.

The egg that was to be the next Great Eagle lay rounded and golden on the table. One by one, after the king, all the people in the room walked past it and gazed at it.

It was the most precious thing in the king's treasury, Antar thought. No one stopped him when he followed the last serving girl. No one took any notice when he stood there. No one stopped him when he stretched out a hand and touched the bright thing.

Only his fingers felt, when he touched, that something inside the egg stirred and pecked back at his fingers, from inside. The egg was beginning to hatch, the young eagle alive inside it.

13

There was nothing Antar could do at that moment. He felt the answering touch from inside the egg, and knew that he had found what he was looking for. Perhaps if doors had been open, the way clear, he might have run off at once.

But the doors were shut tight, the place was full of people, and nothing could be done.

I must pretend I have not noticed, Antar thought. Then no one will know what I think, or guess what I want to do. How long has the egg been hatching? How quickly can I take it away?

The king noticed that Antar was walking about. He was not pleased with that, and gave some orders about it. Two soldiers came for Antar and put him back in the cage. They put the side of it on again and fastened him in once more.

Before they did so they did something that Antar did not understand immediately. One of them took his right leg, lifted his foot from the floor of the cage, and held his ankle for a moment. He did not hurt, or twist, or pull. He smoothed down the leg-feathers in quite a kindly way, and left the king's hall.

The king had his meal. The benches round the table filled with the people who were to eat with him. The serving girls brought plates and dishes round, the cooks sliced meat, and the butlers poured wine from the shining jugs. Antar decided that they were great servants, more important than the people they served.

No one brought him anything to drink or eat. He and the kitten watched all the meats and gravies, soups and sauces, rare vegetables, fine breads, sweet puddings, crisp savouries, being sent from dish to plate, and plate to mouth, and had only the smell.

Antar was being taken no notice of now. The whole company was busy eating, drinking, talking, and no one glanced at him. Then, either the food was all eaten, or it was being carried away, because at last there was no more on the table. Only the jugs of wine stayed, and Antar was interested in them. Every piece of food had gone. The jugs, the cups wine was drunk from, the candlesticks, the relics from the cupboard, were all that remained, apart from some little dishes of sweets that were passed from person to person.

A butler brought the king a dish of raw meat. The king put his hand into it and lifted up a slice. He seemed to say it was just what he wanted.

Then he pointed to Antar's cage, and had it brought to the edge of the table. Its floor was about the same height as the table top. Antar expected that he would be fed raw meat, like a real eagle. He would rather have had something cooked, but he could eat it raw.

The king did nothing for the moment. He was waiting for something else to happen, and had his eyes on the door of the hall. He fingered the meat.

The kitten could not bear to wait. It slid away from

Antar's hand, scuttled across the table in front of the people, managing not to be caught. In an absurd and quite unnecessary way it stalked the meat in the king's hand, then pounced on it, sinking its jaws in, rapidly killed the king's hand when he tried to pull the meat away, shouted a lot of impolite kitten words at him, and dragged the meat back to the cage.

People looked on in horror, because their king had been attacked. The king dabbed his hand with a napkin, then laughed.

The door at the end of the hall opened wide, and the king's children, or grandchildren, began to come in. The king forgot about the kitten, and smiled to see them running towards him.

He said two things. The first meant that the front of the cage should be taken off. The second told the children something about Antar, but Antar did not know what it was. He was busy keeping the kitten in the cage. It was growling and spitting at him, not wanting to lose its slice of meat, and trying to swallow it whole at the same time. Its eyes were like sparks.

The children stared at Antar. He stared back.

A boy made a face at him. A girl put out a hand and pulled at a feather.

The king did not stop her, but told her to wait a little while. Antar did not know why.

Other children complained that he smelled bad. The king shook his head, and seemed to go on to explain that Antar was such a rare bird that a smell or two did not matter. He pointed to the stuffed eagle, to the skulls, to the feathers, and to the golden egg.

The children had a look at those. Then they surrounded Antar from behind, and pulled at his tail feathers. Antar could not feel that very well, but he knew it was happening.

94

They think I am a real eagle, he thought. They think I just have a boy's head. But I am like them, only they are not nice.

They were not kind to him. He had no beak and he had no talons, and there was no way he could defend himself. If he did, he thought, he would be fastened in the cage again, and might never get out.

He was not hurt, but he was teased and laughed at more than he could bear.

I will not cry, he said to himself, and locked his jaw so that it would not move, and held his eyes steady so that they could not flow with tears, and held his throat stiff so that it would not sob. All the same, his forehead grew hot inside, and his knees trembled with rage.

The king brought his plate of raw meat nearer. When he stood up, all the people at the table stood up too, and the meal was over. They left the wine and the sweets, and stood away. It was some sort of politeness in that place.

"See," said the king; or perhaps he said "Watch." He showed the children how to throw meat to Antar. His own throw of a little piece was good. Almost the only thing Antar had to do was open his mouth, and the meat was inside. He had learnt to catch with his mouth, which most boys do not have to learn.

He swallowed the meat. He thought it was beef, but eagles do not get much beef. The children were delighted with that, and clapped their hands when he licked his lips. They felt it was clever of an eagle to manage that.

Then it was their turn to throw pieces of meat to him. Some of them tried to let him catch the meat, but some of them just threw it at him. It was plain that they would rather have thrown stones.

They are not good children, Antar thought. He saw

that the other people in the room were laughing at what was going on, and doing nothing to stop it.

Antar grew angry. He was mostly furious because these things were happening to an eagle, and he was cross too because they were happening to him. He spread his wings and jumped up into the air.

All he did was hit his head on the top of the cage and cross two feathers in one wing. The children thought it was very funny. The king signalled to have the front of the cage brought back ready, in case Antar became too wild. It was not put on at once.

Two things happened next. The doors opened again, and the royal nursemaids came in. They were calling for the children, and were taking them off to bed. The children called to them to come and see the funny bird.

Then the soldier who had held Antar's ankle came back, carrying something that rattled. Antar did not know what it was at first. He did not know his ankle had anything to do with it, even though it was the same soldier.

The soldier bowed and showed the king what he had brought. The king showed the children, and the nursemaids said something that made them all laugh, but which the king thought might be cheeky.

Antar knew what the thing was, and what the nursemaid had said, a moment later.

The nurse had said, "We could do with some of those for the likes of you."

The thing was a chain. At one end of the chain was a ring to fasten round Antar's ankle, where it was bound to fit. The other end could be locked to anything, such as a wall, or perch.

Now the soldier came forward to fasten it to Antar. Antar knew that being fastened by the leg would be worse than being in the cage. He saw there would be no escape once he was chained, and knew that he had to get away at once.

He picked up the kitten suddenly. All the children shrieked that he was going to eat it, but of course he was not. The kitten hiccupped, being full of several lumps of meat that had fallen to the floor of the cage. It was also very sleepy.

Antar stowed it in his shirt, and at the same time stepped out of the cage, pushing through the children and landing on the table. At first he was not clear about what he was doing. He felt it was more important to escape than do anything else.

The children scattered, and the nurses yelled, sure they were going to be blamed. Antar ran the length of the table, knocking over candlesticks, tipping jugs of wine, skipping over a row of eagle skulls, going straight past the egg, and flinging himself off the table end.

He thought he would crash to the floor. If he did he would run out through the still-open doors. If he managed to fly he thought he would do the same.

His wing-tips scraped the floor, a trailing foot knocked the boards, but he was in the air. He lifted on the draught from the door, found a warm current above the table, and flew up into the darkness.

There was not enough light to see the roof from below, but when he was up among the shadows he saw the rafters stretching across the dark, and landed on one.

It was like standing in a tree. Boys may do that, but eagles should stay among rocks, Garak had taught him. There were no rocks here.

Down below there were faces looking at him, and everyone was talking and shouting. The king sent for something, and that something came in at the door.

It was a group of men with guns. Antar saw that he

was to be shot. But the guns were not ready, and had to be loaded.

The nurses did not like the guns, and started to lead the children away. They had to push them, because the big children wanted to see the shooting.

Antar had to act before thinking. All he knew was that something impossible had to be done. He knew it was impossible, because he had tried the same sort of thing before.

An eagle of the true, wild sort can swoop down on its prey and lift it with its talons. Or it can take things with its beak, if necessary. Antar had only his feet, which were not talons at all, and could not hold things. He had no beak, only a small soft mouth. At the moment he had no front teeth at all, because of his age, and if he had they would be no use.

He had to swoop down and pick up the egg with his hands without losing his flight. That was impossible because he used his arms to fly with, and his hands to hold himself up.

He had to do it at once, before the children went out, while the door was open, before the guns were loaded and ready to fire.

The men with guns were too quick for him. They had practised. They did not need to think. They had their guns up and ready while Antar was getting his balance on a rafter. All the guns pointed at him.

Antar dived. He fell straight down to gather speed, and was at table-top height in less than a second, pulling himself along with wings, helping with his feet, like a swan trying to leave the water.

The guns swung down and followed him. All the people from the table screamed and fell to the floor. The king himself dropped out of sight. The nurses panicked and started to drive the children round in circles.

There was not time for much to happen. Antar gathered his wings in front of him, steadied himself with his feet, took the egg in his hands, found the floor coming up towards his chin, kicked, shoved the egg into his shirt on top of the kitten, regained a little height, flew at floor level through the legs of the soldiers, severely thumped several children, and then found himself out in the dark, launched from the steps that led up to the hall, airborne, and getting away.

Behind him light spilled from the hall, and people poured out. There were shouts. There were gunshots. But he was in the air, with the egg.

He had only to fly back, and then he would be at home.

At that moment he crashed into an invisible tree, and knew he had broken his wings, his arms, and his legs, and probably the egg as well.

14

___

He had flown into the middle thickness of a green tree with needles. It had springy, prickly, branches, and they had hurt him with the prickliness, but by being so springy had not harmed him.

He knew his arms were working as soon as he had looked at the kitten. He was sure it was dead, because it lay in his shirt without moving, and it was stiff. But it had eaten so much of the king's meat that it had swelled round, and was still asleep. The crash had not woken it. Antar pulled it out and looked at it in the shadows of moonlight. It yawned in its sleep, and licked its lips.

By this time Antar had found his arms were working, not broken at all, though his skin was scraped. His legs were in order too, and hurting in quite a healthy way. His mouth was filled with pine needles, and he spat them out. He rubbed some tears from his face, and then thought about the egg again.

It'll be broken and dead, he thought. I shall climb down the tree, tear off all the feathers, and stay with the king. I shall get big dinners if they think I am a boy.

Expecting that it would be so, he arranged himself on a

big bough with his back to the tree trunk, and sat firmly. He would wait until morning, he thought.

He brought the egg out. It lay on his hands like another moon, real moonlight shining from it in every direction. It was unmarked, without cracks, uncrushed. It was whole. It stirred in his hands. Something inside it turned itself about, and then tapped on the shell. There was a run of little thuds, like a message in another language.

An eagle, thought Antar, would know what it said.

He heard other noises now. He heard the noise of men shouting in the distance. He heard the rattle of sticks or spears. He heard orders being given and saw lights not far away.

He had hit a tree on a ridge above the river. Under the moonlight he saw the town not far away below him, and the glitter of movement as the gates opened and soldiers streamed out. He saw their faces as they searched the sky.

I am not in the sky, thought Antar. We are up a tree. And he felt like shouting out so that he would be discovered. He felt that he had done as much as he could, and that he would be safest and most comfortable back in the king's hall.

Then he remembered the cage. They will know me, he thought. People always know things like that. They will only be angry.

Their shouts were already angry. Then, all at once, and unexpectedly, there were men down below, looking at the ground, looking upwards.

Antar knew where he was. He could see all round him, though not far into shadows. He was sure the men would look into the tree and see him astride the branch, his feathers tangled and torn, his face scratched, the egg in his hands to show he had stolen it.

But he was in a shadow himself, and the men did not see him. They grumbled, hit the ground with spears in case he was hiding behind a stone or in a tuft of grass, and went on their way.

Antar knew he must go on. He was not sure why. It was something to do with getting his feathers straight so that Garak would not know he had been in a tree. The mountain eagles should avoid trees, and Antar was a mountain eagle. He had to go back to the mountains first, and after that go home.

The only problem was in getting there. Antar stood up on the branch, with the kitten and the egg fastened into his shirt again. He felt his way up to the top of the tree, climbing silently, like a shadow himself. When the tree began to dip and swing under his weight he knew he had reached its pointed top. He looked round.

He was in a place that did not tell him much. He had hoped to see the mountains, because that was where he was bound. Garak had not told him about getting back to where the eagles lived. Eagles know that without thinking about it, and they had forgotten that Antar did not know. They had not told him which stars to follow; and perhaps there were none.

All round were the sides of a valley, with the river washing its way through fields at the bottom. The town itself, with its lights, and more shouts, and squares of roof and wall, was beside the river.

Close by, the river swept its way down a small waterfall, white in the moonlight. Before that the water of the river had come down from the mountains. Antar remembered that the river had lain below him as he came to the town. If he flew along it again it would be a path for him to the mountains. That was simple.

Starting off would be the most difficult part. He still always had to start by going downwards, because his

102

wings were not powerful enough to lift him from the flat ground even when he ran. While he was still in the top of the tree he looked for a starting place. All he could see was a wall of rock beside the river, close to the waterfall.

All round him now there were men searching for him. He had been missed once, but could be caught again. With the greatest care and silence he climbed down out of the tree.

On solid ground, where he could not fall any further, he groomed and preened his wings and tail feathers, brushing them until they gleamed in the moonlight, and every piece of plumage was as much in place as he could get.

The egg and the kitten were safely in his shirt. He slipped through trees and bushes down to the edge of the river.

The water boiled and bubbled at the foot of the waterfall, foaming and heaving at the foot of the little cliff, splashing up in a wind that rose from the water. He did not want to jump from here at all, because one dip of a wing and he would be in the water. An eagle in the water is a drowned bird, and the same is true of a flying boy.

Even though the rising wind would give him a lift Antar thought he could not attempt the flight. The idea seemed hopeless; the water began to terrify him. He was looking round, leaving the edge, ready to go back to the tree, when a man appeared not far away. Antar was just about to run towards him and ask to be rescued from all that was happening, and give back the egg. But the man shouted, first at Antar, then for more men to come.

Antar turned, ran back to the edge and jumped without hesitation. He did not want to be among the people of this town, or to see the king again, or his children, or any of his soldiers; or think about cages and chains on the ankle.

He thought he would die. A true eagle would have known about the air currents, and how they drop down the waterfall with the water. Up the fall was the way Antar wanted to go, away from the place he had jumped from. At that place men were gathering, with bows and spears and a gun.

But that was the place with the rising air. Antar flew round the pool at the foot of the fall, dived into the rising air, and swooped himself up in the face of the men, who had lost sight of him and were peering down the cliff.

They tumbled on their backs and fired arrows at him, and then the gun, but Antar was turning and rising, and out of reach.

He was strongly in the air, high above the trees, circling for height. The river lay below him, and the town, growing smaller as he turned. All at once he felt he was in a place he understood, the sky, doing what he was good at, flying. But he knew he was not so good as an eagle.

He searched for currents of air, all the time watching for the mountains, to check that he was right to fly up the river. He saw them at last, lying off to one side. Between him and them there was nothing but black wildernesses of forest, and nothing to guide him. He decided to follow the river.

Far below he heard men shouting still. He knew he was fully in sight, but out of reach. Then he was out of sight, because he came through a layer of thin cloud spread over the sky, and all the ground vanished, town and trees, and shouts of men, and all he could see was the track of the river, lying like a map of itself in flatness.

He followed it. Gradually it swung itself round until he saw that he was indeed heading for the mountains.

A swift wind came from nowhere and held him, carrying him along so that he hung in still air but the river moved below him, and the mountains came near. He was in some air stream he had not known about, but which eagles would have known and named.

The moon sank down into a lemon-coloured sky, and in its place the sun came up. Down below the trees were full of shreds of mist. Ahead the mountains were made from sheets of lead, like offcuts left from covering steeples.

The sun began to lick Antar and warm him. He moved his wings to change direction a little, because he felt he was getting stiff.

He was now over the mountains. Their peaks and ridges were jumbled far below. Antar looked for a place he knew, where he could meet Garak and the other sentinels and bring them the egg.

They will be glad, he thought. I shall be famous with them.

And there, rising from their high nests, were the eagles themselves, coming in a great gathering towards him, still a mile or two distant.

Antar was full of happiness. He took a deep breath. But something went wrong with the breath. It caught in his throat and choked him. It made him bring his wings in close to himself.

But he could not do that. He was in one of the mountain mists rising from the high peaks, and the mist had settled on his wings as ice and turned them rigid so that he could not move or use them. The same mist had come into his throat and eaten his lungs away.

All he could do was cough, and he did that without being able to help it. It was a cough that twisted his whole body, made his eyes run with bitter tears, and turned him helpless head down in the air.

The kitten drew in some of the same misty air, and

began to scream and splutter. It scratched and scrabbled, having nothing to hold on to. Antar himself was swooping helplessly down the side of the mountain. Not far away the gathering eagles were coming towards him. Towards the mountain from the river men were coming swiftly, pointing and shouting.

Antar could not move his arms. His wings were locked by ice. Then something struck his chin, first something hard and then something soft but sharp.

Because he was upside down the egg had come out of his shirt and was falling through the air faster than Antar. Accompanying it was the kitten. The egg was golden in the sunlight, rotating gently. The kitten was a black blot, claws and tail spread, spinning and somersaulting.

Antar found his wings free at last, and came out of his clumsy dive. But the only thing he could do before he hit the rocks was to turn the right way up, haul himself up a crag, and land on top. Even that was more than his lungs could manage without seeming to burst, and he could do no more. He tumbled over a ridge, and sprawled on the snow of the far side, sliding and rolling down a slope at the broad head of a mountain valley.

Above him the mountain peak wore a golden-red plume of smoke.

Surrounding him, one eye always fearfully on the plume of smoke, came the clan of eagles, watching, waiting.

They are hoping, Antar thought. They think I have the egg.

He stood up, kicking a place to stand in, and looked round.

The eagles were settling in a circle, still watching, all silent.

Garak at last came down closest.

"Where is it?" he asked softly. "Where is the un-hatched young one of the Great Eagle? Did you bring it?"

"Yes," said Antar, in his own language. Then he said, in the eagle language, "It is brought."

"Lay it before us," said Garak.

"It fell from my talons when my wings did not fly me," said Antar.

"You flew into the smoke of the mountains," said Garak. "You have been taught to avoid smoke. Where have you laid the egg?"

"I do not know," said Antar. "It fell out and dropped down."

Garak spoke to other eagles. A group of them rose from the ground and went to look. They knew where Antar had flown, and the egg must lie below that path.

All they found was a hole in a slope of snow, and nothing in the hole. They took Antar to it. He saw that the hole went into the snow at an angle, and had nothing in it, but that it was too small for him to enter.

"You have failed us," said Garak. His eyes went cold and unfriendly. Antar had not seen him look like that. Even the other sentinels, at their least friendly, had not looked like it. Garak looked at Antar and Antar knew he was Garak's enemy.

In every eye of every eagle there was the same look. Antar knew that he had failed and was now about to be killed for it.

Then a man shouted.

15

The first of the men had climbed the ridge of rock, coming straight up, chasing Antar. But he was alone, and only his head showed over the top. Two of the sentinels lofted themselves into the air and went to see to him. The first swooped on him and took his leather cap. He thought the second would take his scalp, and ducked down.

He climbed away and down again, while the two eagles skirmished and threatened over his head. If he stopped for a moment they screamed at him and dived with spread talons.

The other side of the ridge, on the snow slope, Antar was surrounded by the rest. Guarding him to one side was the third unfriendly sentinel, and on the other Garak stood, stern and sorry. He was protecting his pupil, Antar.

"It is my doing too," he said. "I brought this young one up. He has not failed alone."

"He is no eagle," said one of the others. Antar recognized the father of his nest. "He was brought like a cuckoo's egg to us. But he was never a bird. He will never feed himself. I say we have wasted our time, and nothing has come of it. Strip off his feathers, because they are stolen, and let him fly the cliff from the top. That will show what he is. He has been useless to us."

"More than that," said another, "he has failed. We trusted him with the most important thing in all eagle history, and he has not been able to do it, in spite of all we did for him. Now our race will die out because we shall have no leader. Our greatness will become less, and we shall be a laughing-stock like magpies."

"If we let him go," said a third, "he will tell the world all he knows. They will not only laugh at us, but they will be able to find us. Our mountain wilderness will no longer be safe. Already he has brought men."

The two sentinels came back, when they had sent the man to the foot of the cliff.

"There are many men coming," they said. "Gadar has been followed here. He flew by daylight. We shall not live long now. Men will destroy our nests and steal our feathers."

"They will lock us in cages," said the other. "Where we cannot spread our wings. They will feed us meat that drives us mad."

Antar spoke. "The king will give it to them," he said. "I have been in a cage too."

"Be silent, Gadar," said Garak. "Perhaps they will leave you to die, not kill you. That will be fair. You have done nothing for us, and we should do no more for you."

Then a young eagle spoke up, pushing forward to be heard. It was Keek, still smaller than his nest-brothers, but bold.

"I have been in the brood with this stranger," he said. "I do not think he has done well; also he hoarded good food and let it live. But he saved our nest from mountain fire, when the flames drove us mad. He is mad himself, so there was no difference to him. But he has been in the brood with me, even if he came from an egg of some other kind. So I believe we should decide nothing until the Great Eagle has spoken."

Said one of the sentinels, "The Great Eagle cannot come here. You know that he is dying. He will die in sorrow, the last of the Great Eagles. That is all. He may no longer fly."

"He has not been asked," said Keek.

"Go to roost," shouted the other eagles. "Who are you to speak, the youngest and smallest of us all? Are you another sort of stranger?"

Three more young eagles were standing together, uncomfortable, uneasy, looking at one another, pretending they were nothing to do with Keek. But they were from the same brood, and they had some of the same thoughts. Their mother bent her head and spoke to them. "Go forward then," she said.

They came forward. The older eagles had made up their minds, and did not like the young ones to disagree.

"I say they should speak," said the egg-mother. "I cannot say whether or not I agree, but they should be heard."

The biggest of the brood spoke. He was nervous, and his voice was somewhere between a chick-like cheep and the grating growl of a grown bird.

"We do not think he should be killed," he said. "We think he should be left to die. But we think that the Great Eagle should speak."

"And we are going with Keek to get him," said the next in size.

"Yes," said the third, looking round cheekily. His mother flapped him with her wing.

There was a silence. The older birds were looking at one another, deciding what to do.

"We're going," said the eldest of the young ones, raising itself on its talons and spreading its wings. "Where?"

The sentinel on Antar's left spoke now. "I shall go with them," it said. "It was the Great Eagle's choice to bring this animal here. Let him choose now what to do. If he sends a message, that will be enough. Come on, you four, smarten up, get your eyes in, smooth your wings, spread your tail there, and stop looking so pleased with yourself. The Great Eagle will decide about the four of you as well."

The young ones had not thought about that. They set off, beginners wondering what they had brought on themselves, one expert set of wings guiding them and giving orders.

Men were coming on up the steep slope. The one who had come first had had enough by now, and did not lead again. He was washing his bleeding head in a cold stream: one of the sentinels had combed him with a talon like a razor, so he was out of the fight that followed.

In twos and threes the eagles left the circle round Antar and went to the battle. They would fly back in a little while, bringing spears, helmets, arrows, even guns, and drop them in the snow.

"To kill is difficult," Garak explained. "But it is easy to make men helpless, because they go on being frightened of things that are no longer there. Give them one bad night, and for many nights they will expect it again."

More and more trophies were brought. Two eagles flew in with a shield. Antar sat on it, to keep himself out of the snow. He put his feet in a hat.

"They smell of men," said Garak. "Worse even than you, Gadar." Garak was becoming uneasy, not wanting to watch Antar but longing for the battle. "My father fought men," he said. "I have told you he was killed in that fight. Now I wish to give back his death. But I have

111

to watch you, because if I do not then you will either escape, or the others will kill you. It is come to this, that when I could fight I am watching a goose."

And he sulked for a time. Then he did his joking dance and his winking of eyes. "I shall not be miserable," he said. "Perhaps we shall both stay alive. I have told you so much that if you die I shall lose it all."

Antar scratched his neck for him, but Garak could not relax and take pleasure from it. He was anxious all the time about the fight.

At last Antar took one of the spears and used it as a walking stick to help him up the slope of snow. He and Garak went to the top of the ridge and looked down on the fight.

"There are some dead," said Garak.

"Good," said Antar.

"I look only at eagles," said Garak. "Maybe men are dead too. Maybe you are to die also. But stay here, Gadar, and I shall fly down to look. Perhaps this is the last moment of the eagles."

Then he had dropped like a stone down the rock face, fresh and angry, a guided and sharp weapon.

An eagle came up with a knapsack and dropped it in the snow. It broke open and its contents spilt out.

There was bread in it, and cheese, and a lump of cake. In the bottom there was a lump of dried meat. These were just the things that Antar knew of at home, the very things he had missed all the time he had been with the eagles.

The bread was stale and sweet, like honey. It was hard, too, and had to be sucked before Antar's teeth could bite it. The cake was the same, and sweeter still. The cheese was hard as wood. But they were all a feast to him.

Garak came back, and settled to tidying his feathers. "I had to join in," he said. "The men are going, but many of our birds will not come back. One of your sentinels will fight no more, and will never be an egg-father." He looked doubtfully at the knapsack and what Antar was eating. "Eagles do not know what that stuff is," he said.

His eye caught something in the distance, and he gave a cry Antar did not understand. When he had repeated it the eagles came up the cliff from the fight. They formed a half circle this time, because Antar was at the edge of the cliff.

"That is the right place," said one eagle, and another, waiting for the time when he would be thrown off.

But they watched the thing Garak had seen. In a little while Antar could see it too. In the meantime all the eagles round him were setting feathers straight, cleaning their beaks and talons, which had blood on them, and examining their wounds. Some had been pierced with spears; others had sections of plumage missing; there were those with wounded limbs; and one had to walk up the cliff with a broken wing.

Then those that could fly rose into the air again to meet the thing Garak had seen.

The Great Eagle was flying slowly, and all on one side, towards the gathering. On either flank were young ones, and the sentinel flew ahead to make the way easier.

A cloud of eagles went to bring the group across the last mile of sky, and to prepare the ground by clearing away the trophies of battle.

The Great Eagle dropped solemnly down and stood. The sentinel stood close against him, to hold him up. The rest of the birds came back to their places. Keek's mother went across and gave him a peck for causing all this trouble, and went back to her place, looked at by the Great Eagle and ashamed of being angry.

There was a long silence while the Great Eagle recovered his strength. Antar looked down the mountain.

113

Now that the battle had stopped the men had gathered together too. But they were not silent. They were arguing. Most of them were packing and ready to leave, but some were still pointing up the mountain.

"If you attack those that are pointing upwards you will send them all away," said Antar. "The others are going home anyway." It was clear that the men had in fact decided to go home, taking their gear and their wounded with them.

"It is true," said Garak. "But first we shall decide about you. We should send you with the men that go home."

"But they are my enemy too," said Antar.

"It is often so," said Garak.

He said nothing more, because the Great Eagle had asked the gathering to speak. Garak chose those that had something to say. There were many of them, and there was long argument. Antar did not know all the words that were used. He sat on a rock, with his feet still in the hat, and chewed the hard bread.

At last there was silence. Antar looked up to see what the answer was. The Great Eagle gazed into the distance, deciding on it. Now and then his eye fell on Antar.

"Stop eating," said Garak. "This is a solemn occasion. This is a time of living and dying, but not of starvation."

The Great Eagle spoke at last, as the sun was setting. "Some of us are dead," he said. "But that cannot be helped. One eagle or another does not matter, but the race of eagles is important. You are ready to think that this boy-eagle should die because he has failed to do what you intended. But we have never thought of a better way to recover the golden egg. I have lived much more than a hundred years and I am dying, so it is necessary to have another Great Eagle. But you do not know what has happened to the golden egg the boy brought us. You have not asked whether it would hatch. Instead you have been angry, even though this boy has done what no eagle has done, and what no man has done. You should honour him, even if he failed. You are foolish as well as revengeful. You know where the egg is. You saw it fall. I myself, with my old eyes, can see the hole in the snow. What has happened was likely to happen, and perhaps it should happen. I have decided that we shall send the boy down the same hole, and he will bring back the egg. First though, he must lose his feathers."

"Saved," said Garak. "But not for anything better, Gadar."

The feathers were bitten off Antar by Garak and the sentinels. Their beaks nibbled so close to him, but so gently, that he was tickled more than he could stand, and fell down in the snow. The shaven feathers lay at last like a huge haircut all round him; or as if an eagle had exploded on the snow. Antar was led, feeling very naked, to the hole in the snow where the egg had vanished, and told to go down it.

He went, taking with him the knapsack, head first and quickly. The talons that had just been in battle were ready to tear his legs if he did not go, and the beaks began to tap his ankles. He thought he would lie in the snowy hole for a time, then come out and walk home.

But all at once his head went into emptiness, and his shoulders followed. He was sucked into some inner space of darkness and fell down, down, down, helpless without wings.

16

Outside, in the twilight of battle, the eagles stood once more in the snow. One of the sentinels scraped snow into the hole Gadar had gone into, and hid all sign of it.

"It is the end of that," he said. "It is the end of our time."

"We should all have died in the battle," said another, blood in his plumage.

It was time for the living to go to their roosts. All but two could fly from the ground, and those two took wing from the cliff edge and soared home through the darkness.

The Great Eagle lifted himself into the air, but the effort was so great he swooned in his flight, and had to be carried, just as Antar had been carried. He went back to his pinnacle, to be fed in his old age like a new nestling.

On the snow slope there lay the spears and swords of men, their scattered clothing, and the tangled outline of feathers plucked from Antar, muddled and untidy because he had struggled under the tickling beaks.

A cold wind ruffled the feathers, and a dull moonlight gleamed on the weapons of men. All round the ghostly marks of eagle wings on the snow showed where they had stirred the surface.

Antar himself was lost in darkness. He had fallen helplessly through black air, striking some hard places on either side as he went, and finished on a slope that gave way under him. He had slid down the slope, rattling downwards still with it, among small stones, and lumps of ice, and landed on rock.

There he sat, the right way up, unable to know where he was or what he could do.

There were noises all round him. There were creaks, as if someone crept up on him in new boots. But the noise came once from over here, then once from over there, then once from above him. Actual feet walked one foot-step apart so no one was here.

There were enormous groans in the air, as if a building had begun to fall round him. Nothing fell but drips of water. The sounds went on like the anguish of some tormented animal, but there was no animal here. Nothing came to sniff at him, or touch him. He sat on the rock and felt that he was all alone.

The air he breathed felt thick in his chest. His skin felt slippery. He wanted to do nothing but sit where he was.

Drops of water fell round about him. One fell on his shoulder, gripping it with cold. He was used to cold after being in the mountains so long, and ought not to mind one drop more. But this single drop was painful, as well as refreshing.

He realized what had made him feel different. The rock he was sitting on, the air round him, were both warm. In fact, they were more than warm; they were hot. The rock was almost too hot to sit on with comfort. And the drop of water had not been almost ice, but tepid itself. He was in some warm cave, in warm darkness.

Then he found that his hand still held the crust of

bread. He chewed at it a little, then rested. His eyes closed, making no difference to what he saw. The sounds of the place went away, and he fell asleep.

When he woke up there was green light all round him. Now that he could see, he could hear better too. His eyes told him where each sound was, and mostly what had caused it.

He was in the bottom of a cave, but he did not know what sort of cave had a glassy green roof to it, one that leaked drops of water and groaned under its own weight.

Drops of water fell from the roof, and streams of water ran down cracks and fissures, joining into a stream on the rock floor. The stream itself had a little steamy mist above it. When Antar went to drink at it he found the water warm, and in some places hot. Here and there it swirled out of the rock bubbling with heat.

The light was as thick as the heat. It was not easy to see clearly, or to tell whether things were moving. The water of the stream shimmered, rather than flowed, for instance. In the many shadows he thought there was movement.

All round him the place spoke with footsteps that were not footsteps, and animal calls that were some other thing.

Antar went down the slope of the rock, where the rubble had heaped up. Here the small stones had become rotten, and broke under his feet, feeling cold. For the most part they were ice, melting in the heat. But they gradually mounded themselves up until the stream was swallowed by them, and there was no way to follow it.

Antar went upwards again. He thought he could see where he had come into this place, where a hole went up into the roof. He could not get up to it in any case, because the walls of the cave were blue and green and slippery. They were ice, wet with melting.

He came back to where he had spent the night, where the crust of bread lay softening in a pool of water. He ate it, drank a little, and expected someone or something to come and help him. But nothing came, and no one knew.

Antar thought he had fallen asleep again. He was aware again of noises all round him, and the unchanging blue-green light, and the long day lasting for ever. He grew so used to the instruments of the ice orchestra round him that he no longer heard the tunes or the chords. He only heard himself crying.

Now and then he thought he heard Maray calling him, or Roslin telling him something, or Aldect explaining a simple fact, or among the shifting sound of the ice the gritting words of Garak.

He sat with his mind gone away into itself. All that had ever happened to him seemed like a dream. What was round him was so unreal that all other things were unreal too.

His thoughts stopped drifting quite suddenly. In spite of the warmth a cold shiver ran down his back, and he felt his hair shift on his head.

There was a wild screaming close beside him. It was not the ice, but an angry squalling, with growling mixed in with it, and a busy scuffling noise. Antar was terrified because the noise was so sudden.

Then he knew what it was. He looked, and knew where it was. In among some rocks on the floor of the cave was something he knew. He went at once to find it.

The kitten was there, and seemed to be eating some huge thing. It was huge compared with the kitten. Antar saw the kitten's eyes flashing, and heard it snarl and spit.

It was attacking the knapsack that Antar had sent ahead of himself and forgotten about. In the bottom of the knapsack there was dried meat, and the kitten had found it.

119

The knapsack had then seemed to defend itself, with its flap curling round the kitten, and the kitten had uttered loud warnings.

"You are a silly thing," said Antar. He wondered what had happened to his voice, which had become clogged up with gladness on seeing something living and that he knew.

The kitten went on fighting the knapsack, but purred at the same time, making sounds that ought to have warned anything away.

Antar separated bag and kitten. One corner of the dried meat had become softened with wetness. He broke some off, and gave it to the kitten. He ate some himself. They sat together and chewed.

Antar wrapped the meat up again, because it was all he had to live on. Then, with meat in his mouth, he began to think more sensibly about what he was doing.

He was not alone any more. He remembered his duty to the eagles, and why he had been sent down the hole in the snow. Somewhere in here was the egg, probably smashed, with the bird inside eaten by the kitten; but dead in any case.

He had to find it, and be sure. When they had both eaten, the kitten stretched itself out to sleep. Antar picked it up, held the knapsack, and began to look and feel his way about, searching for the smooth shell of the egg.

It was not easy to distinguish such a thing from the smooth ice boulders that littered the cave. The rock itself was often moulded into the same sort of shape and size, and everything was the same colour.

In the end he did not discover the egg by feeling or looking. He heard it. Among the sounds in the place there seemed to be a repeated small clicking thud that was different. When it had happened for the sixth time, and quite near, Antar looked again at a corner he had already investigated.

Lying in a place by itself, and looking like rock, was something, feeling like ice, that made the noise. Inside it there was life. Antar took it on his knees, beside the kitten, and listened for the sound again.

It came again. He heard it, and he felt it with his fingertips. The thing inside, the new great eagle, was pecking from within, not far from hatching.

"We have to get out," said Antar. The kitten yawned, stretched, digging its claws in, and went to sleep again. Round Antar the cave darkened, and night came over it.

Antar sat with the egg on his knees. At intervals it seemed to stir a little. Or sometimes the kitten moved, now and then getting from his knee and going for a walk. Antar himself dozed and dreamed, his back against warm rock, his stomach happy with food in it, and with the thought that in the morning he could see and set about escape.

In the night, on one of its journeys, the kitten seemed to hurt itself. Antar was woken by a screech. He thought at first that the egg had hatched, huge and full grown, and was attacking him, hatred in its eyes.

But it was not so. He saw it was not so, until his eyes watered for some reason. He saw because there was now red light in the cave. The colour, and his own sense of time, told him that day had not come. Something else was giving a light like fire.

The kitten came back, sneezing and squealing. It smelt of scorched fur, and limped into Antar's hands. Antar stood with all his belongings and cares in the same hands, the egg, the kitten, the knapsack.

Something had come into the cave, and was standing at the entrance it had made, and was breathing smoke.

The ground began to shake under Antar's feet. Ice fell

121

from the roof. The thing looked at Antar with an angry eye, and he felt its glance on his skin.

Fire had come in, like a dragon. There was a body of it stretching into the cave, white, yellow, red, and scaled with a black skin. The creature pushed its way in, shouldering through a hole that had not been there by blue daylight. Where it touched the water the water boiled into steam. Where falling ice dropped on it there was a flashing explosion. From the thing of fire there came the strong smell of smoke. Antar felt it burn his throat, just as something had burnt his throat over the mountain when he flew back from the king's city.

The dragon was as much living as anything Antar ever saw. It crept forward, lengthening itself, and putting out legs with burning claws to pull itself along. It came steadily, drying the rock as it came, pushing others aside, squeezing itself from a crack in the floor of the cave; and as it came it roared gently to itself.

Now the cave was no longer warm. It had become hot. Antar retreated among the rocks. Overhead the ice was loosening and falling in boulders itself. One piece, bigger than his own head, rolled against Antar's feet. He put down his handful of things, picked up the ice, and threw it. It rolled off the creature's back, and ended against its snout. It turned the snout black, and stopped it where it was. But as Antar watched, hoping there might be victory, the creature rode over the blackened part, and grew another snout.

Antar had to retreat further. He found his way back into darkness, where ice no longer fell on him, where the heat was not so great. He was in a mound of boulders, clambering over them, finding them loose and ready to fall on him, and hardly daring to go further.

As he climbed on them one became shaken from the others, tipping, hesitating, giving Antar a chance to stand clear while frightening him so much he could hardly move. The boulder, as tall as himself, continued to tip. It lost its position on the pile, and went bounding down. It bounced, with a great report, then landed on the neck of the fire creature, scattering it into the air and across the floor. The boulder settled where it was, over the place where the fire rose from the floor, and killed it dead.

The fire died back, and there was no more of it in that place.

But in another place a new young fire found its way through, and the ground shook again.

17

Fire came out of the ground. It came out of the walls. Here and there, on one side and another, almost surrounding Antar, the red jaws came bursting out. Drops of water from the roof burst against the fires like the snapping and gnashing of teeth.

The cave walls were being dried to vapour where they were rock, and steam rose everywhere. Where there was ice it melted, ran away to some other part of the floor, and turned to mist. There was smoke as well, making the kitten sneeze, biting at Antar's throat. His eyes smarted and tears ran down his face.

All the time the place shook. Mostly the floor merely trembled. Now and then there was a bigger quake, and rocks fell on either side of him, often crushing a dragon of fire to death. But each time the fire came again.

There was so much movement in the floor that he heard it with his ears as well as feeling it with his feet. The rock underfoot became hot, then too hot, so that he was dancing where he stood.

The fires sometimes died away, going back into the rock. When they did there was darkness. But always there was a bigger convulsion in the darkness, and the fire came back stronger.

A long way off there was an explosion. To Antar the effect was of being in a building that was blown up with gunpowder. He was knocked over, and hot air, not quite flame, tramped across him, to be replaced by air that he could not breathe at all.

He was standing up again when he found the air had gone foul on him. He was clutching his throat, and feeling that his eyes were about to jump from his head, when there was another distant noise, and the hot air came back. It knocked him over the other way, scorched him not so badly, and was followed by a very cold wind. The cold wind came driving up through the cave, making him cough again; and his eyes felt blistered.

Fresh air, smelling of snow came like a gale through the passage, chilling him so that he shivered, and turning the heads of fire black as it passed.

But the fires pressed out again, growing from the walls, peering suddenly from behind rocks, lurking in corners, and throwing heat.

Antar was both hot and cold. The wind blew harder and harder. It turned warmer, because it was coming past fire and taking up heat. Antar turned his back to it and walked forward. He could not go back the way he had come, because it was now too narrow.

He was under the ground now, and the roof was rock, not ice. The cave was moving about. It was like being inside the lungs of a gigantic animal, with more passages going to the side, and openings leading off in other directions.

Or it was like being in a chimney, Antar thought, with a huge storm blowing through it or bending the brickwork.

He went where the wind blew, because the smoke gets

125

out at the top of the chimney at last. He hoped the chimney did not start running straight up and down.

Behind him the fire advanced, but not so fast as it once had. He found he had been hurrying, and that there was no need to do so now. He was not dancing alone now, because the rock had cooled underfoot. It stopped twitching too, and round him the long cave grew steady. The noise lessened, and there was an underground peacefulness.

The wind stopped, and there was a sudden silence. Antar moved another step forward, his poor bare feet stumbling on loose rocks and hurting. The small noise that stumble made was echoed from far places, and he knew he was in a bigger cave. But he was in darkness, and could not tell at all what to do.

He was thirsty, and longed to rinse his mouth with cold water. It was full of the tastes of smoke and heat he wanted to be rid of. He would have thrown his mouth away, if he could.

Carefully holding the egg with one hand, the kitten with his elbow, he felt his way to a solitary rock and sat on or against it. He rested the knapsack on the ground, because its strap was irking his shoulder. He decided that he and the kitten were dead, because it was moving its jaws in dry and soundless meows, and he was without hope. He did not want to go home, but wanted to be dead with the kitten where he was.

The egg thumped at him. It was more than a thump. He thought he heard the shell give and grate a little, as if a crack had appeared. He thought that the thing inside spoke a word he did not know, but which was in eagle language.

He looked down at it, knowing he could not see it in the total darkness. But he did see it. He saw its gold

126

tarnished with travelling and tumbling, rubbed with carelessness, and crazed with heat and cold.

It seemed to be giving a light of its own, like a magical thing. But there was another noise with the vision. The noise came from the other side of the place he was in, and showed him where he was.

He was in a huge vaulted cave, the roof like a dome, going into blackness at the far end. At the other side of the cave another dragon of flame was rising from the floor like a solid fountain, casting light, throwing heat, filling the air with smoke again. The smoke went up into the blackness beyond. It seemed to Antar that he was in a hearth, and that the chimney started at the other side.

By this light he saw the egg. It had been spoilt, he knew; nothing could ever come from it now; the noise it made had been its last attempt to hatch.

The fire sank down from its first white and yellow to a dull red, turned black, and sagged into a heap. Its heat pulsed in the cave, and that was all.

The egg remained silent now. It would be so for ever, Antar thought. He felt it with his fingers, and its golden smoothness had gone. It was rough, scaly, and some parts of it might be coming loose.

The wind started to move again, lifting up to the roof. Antar longed for his wings, because he could have flown in this air. All he had of his flying feathers were the stubbly bristles fixed in his jacket and trousers. The smaller feathers on his trouser legs were of no use, just an eagle fashion.

A pure flame jetted up from the middle of the floor, standing as tall as the church steeple, roaring like the sea in a storm, and giving a light that spat and quavered and vibrated, making everything dazzle before his eyes.

The wind grew stronger. Antar's coat flapped against his sides, and he had to move or be torn to pieces. He must follow the chimney to open air, if he could find the way.

The way was clear and dreadful. There was a staggering, crumpled road up the side of the cave.

He began to follow it, picking his way through the soot of this underground furnace, lit by the flickering glow of the flame.

He went up and up. He found he was in the back of the chimney, and able to walk almost where he wished, because the chimney opened wider as he went up it. He knew he would be in darkness when he no longer saw the flame.

He was wrong. As the flame dropped out of sight behind an arch of black rock, other light came from above. It was a red light, and he began to dread getting near it, in case it was more fire, and yet another cave. If so, there would be no way through. He would die of thirst before he managed that.

The light turned blue. It was from the sky. Before the sky had faded to night again Antar was out, over the edge, and on the highest peak of the mountains. Behind him was a smoking hole where the fire came out of the earth in a volcano. Below him were the burnt slopes where fire had recently fallen, and below that the unmelted snows of last winter.

In the distance the rest of the mountains grew darker with night, and beyond them the country of the forests lay already asleep.

Antar slithered down to the snow, scraped off a sooty layer, and put a lump in his mouth. Then he went on down again, feeling the cold of night, wanting to find a shelter that was his own. He hoped he was now free and safe.

At the edge of darkness he came among evergreen trees that grew small at the edge of the snow. He tramped on and on, knowing that if he stopped he would not start again, because his feet were blistered with heat and cold, scraped with rock, torn with rough snow, and black with journeying. He let the kitten swing on the knapsack, chewing a corner of the dried meat, growling and cursing and not a bit pleased.

A rock spat from the volcano had mowed down a cluster of trees, heaping them into a shape like a tent, leaving a scattering of sticks and branches. There was enough light for Antar to make a covering for himself, and to lay down a sort of snowy mattress and a leafy cover. He burrowed into the place, heaped snow over the heap, to become warm again some day. Here were all the things for a fire except the heat itself.

Before morning, while he was asleep, the mountain shook again. Antar felt himself being lifted, complete with his bed and the trees round him. The mountain had a flame standing on it, and rocks were being hurled out burning into the night. That stopped, and there was more noise than Antar could imagine. The top of the mountain exploded into fire and smoke, with lightning and thunder in the cloud. At that moment the sun rose and lit the whole plume of smoke, making the black gold, and turning the whole thing solid.

Bursts of noise leapt up from the top of the mountain, and were hurled into the sky, until they reached their highest level, perhaps where there was no more sky. The noise spread as blackness, out and out, filling the whole of it, and at last cutting out the sun.

In the darkness that followed Antar knew he was sliding down the slope, without knowing where he was going. His bed, and the trees round him, pitched and tossed like a ship at sea, the whole mountainside going to a new place.

In the town the ashes began to fall innocent as a little

white snow on the town green. They began to fill the gutters of the church. They settled out of still air on the roofs and window sills of the town. Those first out thought there was warm snow in the air, and made footprints in it.

But the sun did not rise. The light of early morning went away. Birds stayed in their roosts, and beasts in the fields stood unable to eat or drink.

Lanterns taken outside threw no light. Ashes fell down the chimneys and smothered the fires. The people sat and waited, and the best they could do was clear their roofs, in case the weight crushed the woodwork. Each and every person knew that doomsday had come. They would have rung the church bells, but the bells were embedded in ashes and would not toll.

Antar, far off in the mountains, was clear of the ash, but still he moved. In the afternoon the ash stopped rising from the mountain, and light came back in that place. Antar had come to rest in a quiet valley full of trees.

He dragged the kitten in with him. It still clutched a mouthful of the dried meat, and grumbled at him a great deal. Then it spat out what it was eating, hissed at it, and was suddenly sick, so everything it had eaten recently came out again. Not being fussy about such matters, it started the meal again. Then it stopped, and lay, spread out and still, as if something had gone wrong with it, now and then mewing sadly.

In the town the ashes fell the length of a whole day, from one dawn to another. It was thought they would never stop. For Antar the day became warm and sunny, part of full summer.

The snow round him broke up and melted. He picked up the egg, the knapsack, and the kitten, and moved away from where he was into a little grassy place, and let the sun lie on him in peace. The kitten lay beside him in a very stiff sleep.

Antar slept for a little time too, and woke up with his eyes pale from sunlight. He was hungry now, and broke off a corner of the dried meat and ate it.

The meal was not so good as he expected. There were splinters of bone in it, and a disagreeable taste. He pulled the splinters from his mouth, washed the meat down with water from the stream, and went to sleep again.

He woke up feeling very ill indeed, because of what he had eaten. Like the kitten he was very sick, but instead of falling asleep he had great pains inside himself. Sometimes they curled him into a ball, and sometimes they stretched him out so that he screamed for Maray or Aldect, or for Garak.

The kitten woke and screamed too, calling piteously beside him. And the egg, rolled under a tuft of grass, lay dead.

Antar knew that he and the kitten would die too, and wished it would be soon.

18

Antar woke up, got from his warm bed, and found his foot was bleeding. He had woken up to a sunny morning, and at first everything seemed natural and right. He soon knew that he was not at home, because his bed was dry grass and twigs, scrapings of peat, and tangles of moss. And he could not understand what had bitten his ankle. He thought it must be a bite, leaving a little wound like a deep scratch, with blood in it.

He had been woken from so far away that he had to remember where he was. He did not remember why he was there until something came spiralling from the sky and stood in the grass in front of him.

He knew an eagle feather when he saw it, one of the primary feathers of a right wing. An eagle had been here, buried him in warm covers, pecked him on the ankle, and flown away.

But a moulting feather had fallen from a wing and come down like a message.

Antar was sure it belonged to Garak. He called out in the eagle language that he was watching with Garak. But there was no response from the sky.

Instead, something moved in the grass. It was either the kitten, now standing up unsteadily on wobbly legs, or it was the egg, lying in a tussock, grey and scratched, no longer golden and smooth.

The kitten picked its way down to the stream and drank. Then it sat and washed itself with its tongue, now and then biting at its belly with tiny teeth, where there was a pain. Antar knew about the pain, and had one himself. But he was no longer in sickness and agony, and no longer thought he was dying, or wanted to.

He dusted grass and moss from himself, feeling dizzy after standing up, and sat down on the bed.

Next, he tipped the knapsack over and emptied it of all its contents. He thought the dried meat must have gone bad, and wondered whether he could save some of it. There seemed to be nothing else to eat. He turned the bundles from the sack over with his foot, wondering what to make of them. He saw the splinters of bone up against the meat, but wrapped in something like string, a sort of fluffy cord.

Then several things came together and made a strange sense. The first was that the kitten had hiccups, which made Antar look at it. The hiccups were cured when the kitten jumped into the stream, without understanding about water being wet and that it couldn't walk on it. So it went tumbling over and over in a swift current, recovered itself, swore a little—and came backwards out of the stream tugging a fish after it, and threatening to kill anyone who interfered.

While Antar was watching that happen he was also finding out about the splinters of bone. They were not bone, but slips of wood several inches long, split with a knife from straight-grained pine. He knew what they were, though he had never been allowed to touch them. They were matches. On the ends of the splinters was

133

some other stuff, not wood, smelling disagreeable. The splints had been dipped into this stuff when it was molten and it had dried into a greenish bud. If he rubbed the bud on a dry place it would burst into flame and he could make fire. Of course they were just the things that soldiers might carry in a knapsack.

They had become muddled with the dried meat. In the dark Antar and the kitten had accidentally eaten the tips of several, but there were a dozen left. Antar looked at them with distaste, thinking himself ill again. But all he had now was soreness under the shirt, and a feeling of having swallowed thorns. The stuff of matches was poisonous but, though he had chiefly wanted to die, he did not now think he would.

And the kitten was well enough to catch fish.

There was the possibility of fire, and something to cook on it. Garak had brought small stuff fit to start a fire with, and it was heaped up ready to use.

Lighting the fire took four of the matches. The first crushed itself to dust. The second did nothing. The third cracked and sparked and went out. The fourth turned to flame and sat on the splinter of wood. Antar actually dropped it before he worked out what to do, but it fell into the kindling. In the bright sunshine the flame was hardly visible, but a hole was being eaten in the dried grass and small stalks and twigs, and a thin smoke climbed round Antar's head.

The kitten had started at the tail of the fish while it still flapped on the shore. Kittens usually think they can eat the whole thing quite quickly. It managed to eat quite a lot while Antar gathered wood and made the fire large. When he had done that he pushed a stick through the rest of the fish, from side to side, and toasted it. The kitten sat beside him licking its jaws, and licking them again. It curled up and went to sleep.

The shiny flesh of the fish turned solid and white. Its eyes grew chalky. The cooking took time, and Antar looked further into the knapsack while he waited.

There were gun bullets of lead. There was a jerkin of leather, folded and tidy. There was a short, curved knife. There was a length of twine, and fish hooks wrapped in linen. There was a packet of needles, and a roll of linen bandage.

He ate the fish. He did not want much of it, and it had bones that reminded him of matchsticks and match heads. He had to take each one out carefully and look to see what the spiny thing really was before swallowing the meat. When he had managed to swallow it his stomach thought about it for quite a long time before agreeing to accept it.

The kitten was asleep, its belly round like a ball, snoring gently. Antar felt the fire to one side of him, the sun to the other, and curled up between them. He had a clear picture of going home at last. I shall be a man when I get there, he thought, because of the time that has passed. His thought went on into a dream in which he was more important than home and taller than the church steeple, and Roslin was a small bird that flew round his head.

He was woken by a feeling in his own belly, and felt cold with dread, expecting pain and sickness again. But the feeling was not inside him, and was more of a noise than anything.

He had curled himself round the egg. He had given up any thought about it because it was obviously dead, or bad, or broken. It was an ugly grey boulder now, like part of the rubbish of a mountain, quite without gold, with no sign of life. He had forgotten it had any meaning.

Now it began to make noises again, lying between the fire and Antar. Something inside it tapped, wanting to be

135

out. He thought again that he heard a word of eagle language smothered inside, behind that grimy shell. He was ashamed, then, of the state he had let it get into, and went to dip the linen bandage in the stream and wipe it clean. He grew hopeful, because he felt that he might be doing what he had set out to do. Or what he had been sent out to do.

He cleaned the egg, but made the shell no better. He only rubbed dirt into a network of little cracks and made the egg look a hundred years old.

It might be, he thought, from what the Great Eagle had said.

He went into the woodlands to gather logs, to keep the fire going all night. He decided to eat the rest of the fish when he had done that. He and the kitten shared it while he watched sparks fly upwards into the dusk. He turned the egg so that it was evenly warmed.

Morning came all at once, as if sleeping had used up all the time without letting it actually happen. The fire was small and ashy. Antar raked it together, and looked for the fishbones. They had gone in the night. The kitten was up a tree, with its eyes large and startled, having been frightened by something. There were the marks of teeth on the knapsack, where something had tried to get at the meat.

But the egg lay like a dingy mushroom in the grass, unchanged on the outside.

Antar laid his ear to it. Inside it something breathed. Antar thought that it ought to have been born by now, and be out. He lifted the egg, as if it had been his baby sister Roslin, and held it. It had been lying on cold ground, and he knew that was bad for babies. He knew it was bad for eggs too. At home the clutches under the hens were lying in hay, to hold the warmth and keep off damp.

136

He sat with it in his lap while he made the fire larger and coaxed the kitten down from the tree. Then he took hold of the thought that had been with him since the previous day, when he had woken to find the egg still living.

At the beginning of his sleep he had intended to walk home. At the end of it he had known he would return to the mountains and the eagles, taking them their new Great Eagle. He had received from them very little kindness, but only because they did not think kindness important. But they had given him a lot of attention, and that was important to him. He had grown to think of Garak as one of the most important friends of his whole life. Garak had taught him to fly, had taught him another language, and had given Antar so much of his own self that Antar could not go away with it and give nothing in return.

Also, the Great Eagle himself had come to the gathering on the snow slope and saved Antar's life with his words and wisdom.

Antar held in his hands the thing they had lost long ago, had found once, and lost again. It lay on his knees, rustling inside its shell, moving invisibly, ready to live and be the next Great Eagle.

I shall take it to them, said Antar. I shall take it to Garak. I shall take it to the Great Eagle. Then I shall go home. It will not be long.

There and then a white crack like a river opened in the shell, and closed again. The whiteness was the membrane under the shell, and shadowy beyond the whiteness was the damp darkness of the living thing.

Antar decided to stay where he was, by this fire, until the thing came out. He would then deliver it. Or perhaps Garak would come and fetch it. But staying beside the fire meant that he had to leave it as well, to find something to eat. All he had was the bundle of fish hooks.

He ran one into a finger, then into his knee, then balled up a morsel of meat and baited the barb. He lowered it into a pool of the stream, as his friends had done in the river at home.

When I get back I shall go to school, he thought. I shall do anything my father wants, and anything my mother wants, and most things Roslin wants. But these thoughts were more like a promise of things if he managed to catch a fish.

He caught three fish with the same blob of meat. They faded on the rocks beside him, ice-cold from the water. It came from the snow, he thought, looking up the valley to where the white peaks closed it in. He knew he would have to go up there soon, if the egg hatched a young eagle.

He built the fire again, and cooked the fish as Maray sometimes did, hanging them in the smoke. With the knife he gutted them first. The kitten was very happy with that part as its meal. Antar ended up with a meal, and a fish and a half left for the next one.

Early the next morning he woke up, reaching his hands down to the egg, to see whether it still lay there, whether it had opened in the night to let the chick out. He stretched out slowly and sleepily, hardly moving.

So he was awake as soon as something pecked at his ankle, and sitting up looking as it flew away.

It was Garak, perhaps, he thought, with a primary feather missing either side. But why Garak? He rubbed his ankle and puzzled about it. Surely it was Garak?

Being pecked on the ankle meant that he had to move. It had happened to him many times in the nest, and before he reached it. Before the eagle ranged out of sight

Antar called out, in Garak's language, Garak's own name.

"Gadar, Gadar," came back the cry from the sky.

And from much closer, the eagle name, "Kekayakan," shrill and sudden, as startling as if the kitten had shrieked it.

19

The shout of "Kekayakan" came from the egg. The kitten watched it with a great deal of suspicion, because it had put out a foot, hooked and sharp, through a crack in the shell.

The crack opened wider and further, and a head came out, dark and moist, looking round for something to peck at. The young eagle, the young Great Eagle, was hatching itself. It put its head in again and worked with its beak at the shell it was leaving. It broke the two halves apart, and rested, bringing its head out again and drooping it on the shell.

The damp down on its neck began to dry. It was not fluffy at first, but in little spikes, not yet white like the other eagles.

It was a young eagle, with a young eagle's beak, and very clearly an eagle's eye, seeing far and knowing much even when it was only minutes old.

Antar did not know whether to help. Now the bird was hatched and living he had only to deliver it, and he would be able to go home.

Today, he thought. I shall do it today. And he called for Garak, but Garak had gone.

He laid his hands on the shell, to pull the halves apart and release the creature. He was immediately thumped on the wrists by the bird, who considered he was something to eat. It looked him in the eye, proudly like a prince, and screamed "Kekayakan" at him once more.

It watched him. Antar watched it. The kitten sat apart from them both, unsure how things stood.

"I'm going to take you to the eagles," said Antar. "I'm going home. I'm tired of all of you. I just want to do nothing."

The bird waved its head at him, hunched its shoulders, and strained at the shell. It was not free of it yet. Already it knew how to be an eagle, with that way of looking, and the manner of holding its head.

"Nothing," said Antar again. But there was a great deal to do before that nothing could happen. He had to work out how to do it. He was not only looking after himself and a kitten, but he had a bird not quite hatched.

"We're going," he said.

"Kekayakan," said the bird, stretching up its throat, opening its beak great and yellow inside.

The kitten went into the knapsack, on top of the leather jerkin, with meat, matches, needles and fish hooks safely below. The knapsack went on one shoulder. The fire stayed where it was. Antar sat beside it to eat the last of the smoked fish, then dropped the bones on the embers. He picked up the two halves of the egg.

They were still joined together by the bird inside, which either fitted it snugly, having been brought up there, or was somehow joined to it. The eggs Antar had had most to do with he had eaten with a spoon, and they had contained only white and yolk and some speckly

141

bits he left on the side of his plate. This was the first with a living thing in it.

The living thing pecked at him, trying to swallow his arm. But it was very young and comical.

It had to be taken to its own kind. Antar left the fire and walked up the valley beside the stream. He had come down this way and knew what he would find. He came upon the slide of hillside that had brought him from the mountain top. It had filled the valley with a heap like the face of a dam, and water trickled down from the top.

Antar climbed up on the side away from the mountain. When he looked up he could see smoke hurrying from the summit; when he looked down he could see just a little smoke rising gently from his own fire.

He hated going up into the mountains again. He knew that home was far, far below, on the land at the edge of the sea. He knew that somewhere the stream he was beside would reach the sea, and he wanted to walk down it and find himself among houses and people and eat sweet things.

The ground turned again to snow under his feet. Now there was nowhere to put the egg down even for a moment's rest, and nowhere to rest in any case.

The mountain top disappeared. The valley below went out of sight. A cold snow-mist drifted round Antar and his burden, the sparks of dazzle were green and red in his eyes.

He walked on. The mist grew colder and darker. Underfoot the mountain now and then shook, and the air rumbled.

"Kekayakan," shouted the bird. The echo came back from crag and cliff. Antar heard it, and wondered whether there wasn't a touch of something not just echo,

142

something like the true call of another eagle. It did not come again, and Antar was not sure enough to call back.

The egg, and the bird, writhed in his hand. It managed to rid itself of half the shell, and now had two clawed feet to hold on with. The other half shell was still round its rump, like baby clothes.

He either walked out of the mist, or it went away, because it was no longer round him. He saw night falling, and sunset on the high peaks, and round the jagged edges saw the circling eagles miles away.

Before darkness was complete he tipped the litle cat from the knapsack, pulled the jerkin over himself, and put the eagle in the bag instead. It was no longer possible to call it an egg. Somewhere back in the snow half the shell lay forgotten. The bird closed its eyes, and the kitten complained.

Antar had no one to complain to. He was disappointed at coming through the day without getting rid of his burden. He had walked far, and high, and found no eagles, and none had found him. He had wanted most of all to be walking home by now. He would do that day and night, he knew, day and night without rest.

He did not start home the next day either. He sat under a rock through the darkness, and the darkness was not long because now was midsummer. For breakfast he ate dried meat and a drink of water from a small stream. To get to the meat he lifted the eagle out of the knapsack, and had his knuckles rapped for doing so. The other half of the shell stayed in the knapsack and appeared useful.

The bird was hungry. It shouted its one word at him, "Kekayakan, Kekayakan," until it saw what he was doing, which was cutting a wedge of dried meat for himself. The bird snapped at it, took it, and swallowed it

143

greedily, gulping and gaping to get it down, and then stood on his arm breathing noisily.

Antar thought he had killed it, and that it would choke in a moment or two. If that happened he knew he would go home at once, and forget everything that had happened, because he would have failed.

Before long the bird breathed more naturally, and sat with a sort of smile on its face, comfortably full up, not overstuffed.

Meanwhile the kitten wanted food. After that Antar had some for himself. The half shell made the first cup he had used in a very long time. He filled it with water and drank from it.

He walked on. I am this bird's nest, he thought. It perches on me.

Its claws dug into him. It walked up his arm, over his head, down the other arm. It tweaked his ears and looked up his nose. It stared close into his eye and shrieked at him. It looked very sharply at the kitten, knowing as eagles do that it was food. But it could not walk to the ground from its nest of Antar.

In the afternoon Garak flew overhead. He said, gently, "Gadar, you are in the watch of Kendor. Here you must not catch food. I shall bring you something but feed the young one hastily."

"Take the young one," said Antar. "I have brought it to you."

"I am your sentinel," said Garak, rising on the wind. "You must bring him to others. Fly well."

He was out of earshot. But the young eagle was in a tempest of rage at Antar for speaking to Garak, and angered because Garak had come near but brought nothing. Antar had to stop walking, cut meat for it, and feed it small pieces. At his back, watching from on high, was a

144

bird he did not know. He supposed it was Kendor, jealous of his watch.

At the edge of darkness Garak brought the hind legs of some mountain animal. He dropped the food close by. "Bring the young one to the nest," he called softly, and winged his way down the slope close to the ground, to get himself from Kendor's watch.

There was a battle about the feeding. The young one had to tear the food for himself, but did not want to touch the ground while it did so. Antar, of course, did not want to be the plate on which the food was savagely ripped apart. Between them there was a fine tantrum. Antar had to hit back now and then.

After the meal the bird, now smelling, like other young eagles, as if it had gone bad, climbed up on him and went to sleep under his jerkin. It was a large jerkin and there was room for it but Antar wished there were no claws.

Another day was gone. The next could be the last in the place. Antar began to know the peaks round him, could see the pinnacle of the Great Eagle, and recognized the cliff behind his own nest. All day long the eagles circled high above, kept at a distance by Garak and the other sentinels, only coming closer as he came nearer to the nest.

When at last he came to his old hearth, and drank from his old tumbling stream, and found the nest empty in front of him, and heard the wind rising beyond, he thought he was at a sort of halfway home. It was a place he knew and understood, where he had sometimes felt a little happy with Garak; but sometimes as miserable as it was possible to be.

The eagles gathered on the cliff. The three remaining sentinels ringed the nest. Overhead others came and

145

went, interested in what was happening, but uneasy about something too.

"Bring it here, Gadar," said Garak. "This is to be its nest."

Antar came into the nest and set the eagle down on its surface. It immediately killed an old bone, and then shouted for food at the top of its voice.

"Gadar's mission is done," said Garak. "He shall go home."

"Send the goose home," shouted the others.

"Kekayakan," shouted the young bird.

"Which pair of birds will bring the young one up?" asked Garak. "Come forward and let him know you."

There was a wait now, and some quarrelling on the cliff and overhead. Then two birds came forward to the edge of the nest and spoke to Garak and the other sentinels. They were shy about what they were to do, and tended to walk backwards while they spoke, a sign of embarrassment in eagles.

They had brought food with them, and laid it on the nest while they spoke.

"Gadar should leave now," said Garak. "These two will take on the task now. They have been chosen to brood the Great Eagle."

Antar went away. The young bird followed him, making a saddened noise. Antar took no notice, glad to be out of reach of the sharp little claws and the screaming voice. He clutched the kitten and the knapsack and retreated to his hearth. He had done his work and wanted to be on his way.

The young bird followed him, its legs still not long enough or strong enough for walking far. It waddled towards him, looking at no one else. One of the two new birds came in front of it, to act as its parent, but was knocked down and trampled on. The food it brought was ignored.

The same thing happened to the other bird. The young eagle had eyes only for Antar.

"It will forget," said Antar. "It will know it has to be an eagle." He had seen it knowing that already, so it could not think it was a boy.

"It does not think it is a boy," said Garak, after a few more attempts to make it know its new parents. "It thinks Gadar is its egg-mother and egg-father."

"I have not laid an egg," said Antar. "I have found it and carried it, that is all."

He said it many times. There was angry quarrelling about it. But all the time the young bird stood in front of Antar asking for food, treating him as its parent. Other eagles circled, or flew away, and there was much going to and fro overhead that Antar did not see or understand.

"You did not bring us the egg," said Garak. "You brought us the new Great Eagle. One feather is not another feather. Matters are not the same. Gadar, you have become the egg-mother and the egg-father, and it is necessary for you to stay and brood this young eagle. You will have to do it, because no bird here will allow you to leave alive. Yours is the task. You must live with this young one. No doubt that was what the Great Eagle intended."

"O Garak," said one of the sentinels, flying in from an errand, "on hearing the news the Great Eagle himself flew to the sky for ever. It is his wish that his feathers grow on this boy, who shall bring up the new Great Eagle."

"So you shall stay," said Garak. "We do not know for how long. Here is the nest. We are your sentinels still."

And with a hundred eagle eyes on him Antar knew he

147

would not be allowed to leave until the task was finished. This was all the home he had; and, somehow, these were his people. "It is right," he thought, but with tears on his face.

20

The young bird was called Kekayakan. It had named itself with its first word.

"It is always so," said Garak. "Is it not? A pity your
first word was goose, Gadar."

Garak was on the edge of the nest, and had just
brought a hare for Kekayakan. There had been a fight, as
there was each day, when Antar took the animal first and
used the knife from the knapsack to cut himself a section
of meaty back. He was used to nest-keeping now, and
both he and Kekayakan were being fed as much as they
could eat, and sometimes more.

Antar had made his fire again with one of his matches.
He cooked on it, and sat against it at night and when
cold winds blew. But for the most part the weather was
fine.

The young Great Eagle had fluffed out into having a
pure white coat of down, thicker than usual.

"He will have longer feathers than other eagles," said
Garak, "as you know, Gadar."

Antar knew. The old Great Eagle had been at the end
of his moulting when he flew into the sky for ever, and

his feathers had been saved for Antar. Now, if he was not feeding Kekayakan he was tending the fire, or sewing feathers into the jerkin. His own clothes were too worn and ragged now, and the jerkin, though very large, was new. He had little time to think about going home, or to be sorry he was not there.

He had had to trim the ends of the sleeves off, but the rest was ready for feathers. He had a knife and real needles and fishing twine, and could make a tight job of it. Gradually he grew his own feathers, and waited for Kekayakan to grow his.

"Shall I go home then?" he asked Garak.

"I have promised before and been wrong," said Garak. "But I think it will be so this time. Unless you wish to stay in the company of eagles and watch your own territory, and brood a nest."

"Will they let me go?" asked Antar. "This nest is enough."

"I think they will let you live," said Garak, walking backwards and flying away. That was all Antar could get from him.

Not knowing more about the future made the long days longer still, but the way Antar's days were filled made them shorter too. He seemed sometimes not to rest, with the demands Kekayakan made on him, with looking after himself, and with growing feathers, if it could be called that. Eagles grow them without thinking, but Antar had to lay each one in place, then sew it down through the hard leather, and pull the twine tight. If the kitten had not played with the end and tangled it beyond loosening.

Kekayakan did not seem in a hurry to grow his plumage. He ate, and he bullied Antar, trampling on him, pecking him, shouting, taking his food, threatening the kitten; and he ate again, without any ending. Antar cleaned up after him, pushed food into his mouth, if that was what Kekayakan wanted, or threw it at his feet and let him worry it apart. He brought him water in his own mouth, he brooded him warm at night.

He could not teach him all the things that a true egg-parent knew, like the names of other birds, or of places, or how the winds were likely to blow. Kekayakan knew how to understand those things, but he had to be told by an expert.

Garak was the expert, as patient with Kekayakan as he had been with Antar. Antar, sitting close with his sewing, listened and learnt, or sometimes had to put everything down and peck with his hand at the young bird to make it listen.

"Thank you," Garak would say later. "There is much to teach him, but he learns. There is one way in which you are different, Gadar. With you, sometimes you have said things that made my feet walk up and down on their own, and forced my eyes to close. Eagles do not know much of laughter or of friendship, but perhaps they were what I experienced."

Antar scratched Garak's neck for him until the kitten was jealous.

Day after day, and probably week after week, the young bird's down refused to turn into feathers. There was no row of dark signs on the edge of its wings, no quills unfurling beneath its skin.

"You will have to sew them on," said Garak, making a joke himself. "No, this is a great eagle, and it has to grow larger and that takes longer."

"They want me at home," said Antar.

"We need you here," said Garak. It was so. Antar was watched all the time, mostly by the sentinels, but by other birds too. I know I am not at home, he thought.

They know it as well. They know I shall run away as soon as I can.

Once he had wandered a little way from the nest, following the kitten. It was not safe for it to go far away, because eagles cannot help eating things that size, tasting like kitten. It had been safe among rocks, but Antar had been buzzed and pecked until he came back to his hearth, and scolded after that when he had put smoky stuff on the fire. His ankles had bled again, where beaks had nipped him.

The kitten had come back on its own, its ears flat with terror.

There was going to be no escape until the right moment. That was clear. Whether he would ever get away was not clear at all.

Kekayakan grew taller than Antar. He could stand on the nest beside him and look into Antar's eye. He was strong, too, though not heavy. He could bully Antar as much as he liked, and often did; but he always understood that he was its egg-mother, and obeyed in the end.

One day Antar looked at him and began to think he did not look right. He had grown ragged and untidy. His down was coming off in patches, and he was getting bald between the eyes. His eyes were fiercer too, and his beak different—it did not open so wide now, or seem impossible to fill.

His down was falling away, because feathers were beginning to bud, showing dark in the skin below, in rows along the wings and across the back.

He grew bald between the eyes because the beak was becoming different and growing larger. It was from the marks between the beak and the eyes that Antar knew which eagle was which. He knew Garak without thinking about it, and could tell the other sentinels from other birds and from each other.

Now he had an eagle that was growing up and learning. He became more thoughtful as the feathers emerged. They came quickly, getting larger almost as Antar watched, arranging themselves as they should be without Kekayakan having to do anything about them at all. They formed up naturally neat.

Antar hurried with his feather-stitching. He had his wings ready, but the tail was causing him problems. He had to wear the cut-off pieces of sleeve on his legs and sew feathers to them. But he did it. One day he had all the flight feathers sewn down tight, and had only to mend the gaps in the small feathers on his trouser legs.

Each small feather took a long time to place and sew, with the needle becoming harder and harder to push through the leather. But he kept up with the legs of Kekayakan, who was losing his fluffy legs and beginning to wear his own bronze-coloured trousers. Also he was beginning to strut about and be important, exchanging calls with other eagles, and being quite impertinent to the three sentinels.

"He is only a child until his first flight," said Garak. "So far he can only jump up and down."

So far that was all he could do. But when Antar had fledged himself he felt it was time to show Kekayakan how to use real wings. He had not flown himself for a long time now, but he knew how to do it, and was ahead of Kekayakan.

His first flight now was a running glide from the nest to his hearth, with the wind just filling his wings and holding him up, allowing him to land almost as he wanted.

The kitten was terrified. It had not expected Antar to turn back into a thing that eats kittens.

The next day Kekayakan lifted himself into something better than a jump, and hovered in the wind a yard above the nest for several seconds, longer than could be managed just by jumping.

A puff of wind blew him on to his back. Antar laughed, but Garak came at once to see whether Kekayakan was hurt. Kekayakan had got himself up and groomed his feathers back into place.

"Do not forget, Gadar," said Garak severely, "that Kekayakan is our Great Eagle, even if he is only a nestling to you. Parents have a great responsibility. I know, because this year I should have been an egg-father, if I had not had to be your sentinel. It is because you were to come here that I have gone without my brood of eggs."

"I think I have been your brood of eggs this year," said Antar. "You have brought me up instead; and you have become egg-grandfather to Kekayakan."

"I had not thought of that," said Garak. He went away and gave Kekayakan a tweak or two to smarten him up and show who belonged where in the family.

That night, when no one watched him, Antar flew round the nest. His arms had forgotten the work, and he found they tired very quickly, and became painful. But it was coming into his mind that he knew what to do, and when to do it. He had been with the eagles long enough to know when they would not be watching him.

While he was still flying he tripped over a rock and crashed. He had an interesting cut on his knee from that. The next night he sideslipped into the cliff, not quite able to manage climbing up the wind. He felt he need only practise to become skilful again.

The kitten did not think of flying. Antar sorted out some feathers left over from his own wings, and then decided it was no use making any for a cat. He had never heard of a cat that flew, he told Garak.

"And a boy certainly could not," said Garak, with one

154

of his beaky smiles. "Equally, you must not use the Great Eagle's feathers on a food animal."

The time began to come when Kekayakan was almost ready to fly on his own. It was hard to keep him on the nest. He would flutter and fan round Antar's head when Antar was cutting up some meat. It was like trying to live inside a feathered umbrella in a mad wind, with wings thundering, talons grabbing sharp, and beak thudding hard, and great screaming in his ears the whole time.

"I hate you," said Antar at last, one day, when Kekayakan would not stop, and was clawing at his face, determined not to let Antar have anything to eat for himself. "I hate you," he shouted, snatching away the small dead animal, a squirrel, and throwing it over the edge of the nest, down the ten thousand foot precipice.

Kekayakan stopped fighting, looked round and round the nest for the food, and went to sulk in the middle of it, glaring at Antar with his eyes hooded in anger.

"I don't care," shouted Antar. "I don't care any more. You are a rotten eagle, and I hate being your egg-mother and I wish I had dropped you in a river or thrown you into the dragon fire, or the king had boiled you for his tea." He stamped off, and sat beside the fire, not able even to talk to the kitten.

Then he spent a miserable night, hungry, wishing he had not lost his temper quite so much, sorry for Kekayakan without a proper mother, and wondering what he could do to put things right.

Garak was waiting for him at first light. He talked to Garak about his unhappiness.

"You are not the worst egg-mother there has been," said Garak. "I hear that in some nests, but I won't mention any names, the egg-mothers eat the last eggs, if there are more than two. It's one thing eating other birds' eggs, but your own are a different matter. And really,

Gadar, you are the most good-tempered bird I have ever met. Most egg-mothers are in a furious temper all the time. It's quite natural, because young eagles are quite unreasonable, and some of them are quite mad for food."

"All the same, I am sorry," said Antar.

"It is time to do the next thing," said Garak.

"I shall not do the next thing, whatever it is," said Antar. "I shall go home. You have promised."

"Have I?" said Garak. "But this is what you must do."

And he told Antar what it was. "Oh," said Antar. "Yes."

That day he did it. When the sun had risen some way he went to the nest, woke Kekayakan, made him walk to the edge by the precipice, and then pushed him off, and watched him fall. It had been time for that, Garak had told him.

Then Antar himself followed. That was what his new wings were for, just as Kekayakan's were.

Kekayakan opened his wings, spread his tail, and was flying as if he always had.

But Antar was tumbling down and down, as if he never had, head over heels, and his wings and tail were unable to hold him up. They were now too small and too weak, because he was too large and too heavy. And perhaps Garak had not been able to promise he would go home, because this last flight was all that was in store for him.

The world spun round. The clouds halfway down the precipice came towards him; and below them the rocky forest waited in shadow to catch and kill him.

21

Antar had been hurt, long ago, when the Great Eagle had let him fall and the four sentinels had taken him out of the sky. This time, when he had jumped into the empty air on his own, purposely, he did not mind the talons that grasped his wrists and ankles. The nipping pain was safety.

Garak had come suddenly on his right side, spinning and turning with Antar. On the other side was another sentinel; and somewhere behind, the third. Their talons closed like steel and held him safe, steadied him, flattened out the whirling landscapes of sky and mountain, and he felt he was saved.

"We cannot hold you ourselves," said Garak. "You are too heavy now, and we are fewer. We can only help. Your own wings must fill with air and let you glide."

"We shall let you go if we cannot help you," said the other sentinel.

"But if you fall we shall not eat you," said Garak kindly. "We know you would not like that."

Antar tucked his head in, arched his chest, raised his shoulders, balanced himself. In mid air, with the ground still coming up towards them all, Garak walked along his arm and held him above the elbow.

"Use your holding feathers," he said. He meant Antar's wrist and hand, and fingers, the things he felt the air with.

The other sentinel dropped away, and then held him across the back. Garak took hold of both arms, stretching himself across to do so.

Now there were six extra wings supporting Antar, and he found that his own were beginning to hold the air. It began to move less fast through his feathers, and the ground held itself away. He was no longer falling. He tried to fly upwards, to get into the rising air and be at the top of the precipice again.

"Do not fly upwards," said Garak. "We cannot hold you long enough. You must fly to the ground. All we can do is let you land softly."

Antar was thinking anxiously that he would have to walk right up the mountain again, perhaps further than he had the first time he came. He hoped that his ankles were not to be pecked at all the way.

He came down to a clearing among the trees, and flew the last few yards on his own, making a good landing and staying on his feet. When he turned, pleased with that, he looked up and saw the mountain rising sheer to the height of the nest, clear of cloud, and with the specks of flying eagles at the crest. He felt so dizzy with the distance that he knelt down and held his head. Persons with long tail feathers do not sit down often.

"We let young eagles fall if they do not fly at once," said Garak. "That is the way of strength. But Gadar was not meant to fly, and only did so to help Kekayakan. Men are foolish, we know. Gadar, you look like a bird, but are only a goose."

Antar opened his eyes. Two eagles faced him; and then

158

the third sentinel flew down and stood in the grass too. He spoke to Garak.

Garak said, "Gadar will wait here. He is now on his way to his own nest and will not climb the mountain again. He will soon see his egg-mother again. But he must not go yet. Something is coming for him."

"My kitten?" said Antar. "I want my kitten. And my boots? They are on the mountain."

But there was no answer to either question. The eagles left him, spiralling up the straight side of the mountain through cloud and shadow. Antar waited. He knew Garak would bring the kitten, but did not expect the boots.

A cloud of eagles fell out of the sky all round him. Most of them looked at him, first one eye then another, but some stood watch against the forest round them. Last of all came the young Great Eagle, Kekayakan, no longer a tiresome fighting creature on the ground, but a huge soaring bird, knowing how to be an airborne eagle before everything else. He was escorted by two sentinels. He came to the ground like the others, and approached Antar.

Antar generally expected to be knocked over when Kekayakan came near. But Kekayakan was like a prince now, tall, glistening with new feathers, and lord of every eagle in the ranges.

He spoke one word only. "Gadar," he said. Then he bowed his head in front of Antar, to show that he owed him his life. Antar dared to put out a hand and scratch the Great Eagle's neck. Kekayakan turned his head round and held Antar's wrist, like a handshake. Then he stood up and walked away, a prince over men as well as eagles. The other birds bowed their heads to Antar, and all rose into the air together. The pressure and brushing of their

159

feathers made the trees sway as they went upwards, and Antar was alone once more.

The eagles lofted themselves into the sky, spreading like smoke, and dispersed.

Antar waited still. He had not been told to go. His work had been done, and he must be free to leave. Yet he had no idea which road to take, because one way led to the mountains, and all others away. He did not know which was homeward.

Garak was beside him suddenly.

"Have you brought my kitten?" asked Antar.

"No," said Garak. "I shall catch food for you on the way. I am to see you home. The other sentinels will help me."

It was no use to tell Garak about liking animals as pets. He had no idea about that at all. "You did not need to eat it when you were in the mountains," he said. "You certainly won't need it now."

Antar walked. He felt perfectly safe. An eagle as your watchdog keeps every enemy away, and sees trouble far ahead. If he sees a bear, or a hunter, wolf or robber, the eagle is not seen himself. So Antar did not think about dangers all the way, and did not know what he had avoided.

The sentinels were more cautious than they need be. They would not let Antar walk near any house, or along any road. He had to pick his way through the forest, clearing by clearing, avoiding the rides. He had to walk the long way round villages.

Now and then he smelt hot food, or the tang of smoke from house fires. The eagles avoided smoke most of all, from mountain fires or chimney tops.

The mountains grew lower behind Antar. For several days they grew smaller, then after that they seemed to sink a little each day, until they were only a fringe at the bottom of the sky.

Now the eagles had to roost in trees, because there were no crags. Once or twice they allowed Antar to approach buildings, but they were always ruins, and he did not know what they had been when they were new. He ran about the first one he came to, shouting to be let in. But all the doors had long gone, the windows been broken away, and the roof scattered by storms. Trees grew in its hearths, and wild flowers across its floors. That night its gable ends were watched over by eagles, while Antar curled himself at the foot of a decayed staircase.

Once or twice they travelled by night. "We are not owls," Garak said, "but we are not blind." They crossed a bridge over a wide river. Antar did not know where they were at all, and this river was wider than the one he knew. He hoped they were not coming to the city of the king, where men were looking for a boy dressed in feathers.

At the bridge only one child looked from the toll-keeper's window and saw four great birds step in silence across at midnight. She put her head under the covers again, and thought she had seen the bridge itself dreaming.

Again by night, they came across a sleeping circus that had pitched its tents ahead of them since one of the sentinels looked at the way ahead. The captive birds of the show woke up and called to their free cousins, and the beasts stirred in their cages. And from one box of bars came the cry of a mewed mountain eagle imprisoned there.

There was pity from the wild eagles, who did not want to leave one of their kind locked up for show. They swung their flight to the wagon that was its aviary, and spoke with it, using more words than Antar knew. Then, with more caring than Antar knew they had, they tried to tear the iron bars down, and were unable to do so. Their talons rattled and slid on the cold metal, and their beaks tapped and wrenched, with no effect.

"One of our kind is locked in the steel egg," said Garak. "He cannot spread his wings."

"He has no land to watch," said one of the others.

"Wait," said Antar. "Stand back."

"Your hands are softer than our talons," said Garak.

"But he has the skills of a squirrel," said another.

"There is no lock," said Antar. "There is a chain with a pin driven in. I shall pull it out."

But the task was beyond him. He had to make Garak pull and pull, until the pin loosened, and then could be lifted away.

With day coming closer and closer, with men stirring in their beds, and fires being lit, the pin came out in Antar's hand.

He bent back the chain, which had not been moved in a long time, and pulled the door open.

"Come out," said Garak, to the bird inside.

"I am afraid," the bird said. But at last it stepped to the threshold, spread its wings, flew to its own roof, and plunged up into the sky with a wild cry of farewell.

Antar's eagles flew in the faces of the men coming from their beds at the sound, and the men did not know where to look. They would have caught Antar, who looked very like an eagle to them, but when they found what friends protected him they left him alone.

One day Antar came to the top of a hill, and saw an apple orchard. He climbed a tree to get a high ripe apple and see what was ahead. When he did so he saw a shining thing and knew what it was. It was the gilded cross on the steeple. Below it there was the ball, and below that the spire, but the tower itself could not be seen.

But it could be heard. Antar knew the day, for the first time since he came away. It was still Sunday, and the bells were calling for church. If he hurried, he thought, he might be there for the service, because the five-minute bell had not begun yet.

He came out of the tree and began to run, but he was too far away, and could not get there in time.

"Is there danger, Gadar?" called Garak.

"It is my home, my nest," Antar called. "There is no danger here."

"Wait," said Garak. "We watch for danger to ourselves also."

"You are safe with me," said Antar.

The only one to come with him was Garak. The two others turned back. "They have gone back to their nests too," said Garak. "You are not the only one to have been a long time away, Gadar."

Antar was walking and running now. It took him all day merely to reach the next night, and then he had to stop. He slept in a stack of hay, with Garak in a tree and rather ashamed of it. When light came in the morning he hurried on once more.

He came into a road, and went along that. Garak was unhappy about roads, preferring the free ways of the sky. "You will meet people," he said.

"Good," said Antar. He wanted to meet everybody. When he came round a corner he had to stop, all at once, because ahead of him lay the town, dusty with ash from the mountains, bedraggled with soots from that fire, but still his own place. The church stood under its golden cross; before it was the town green, and beyond that his own house.

"That is it," he told Garak.

"It is a wooden egg," said Garak, thinking it was a cage of some sort, not a properly built nest.

Antar walked and ran to the edge of the green. There, in his excitement at coming home, he spread his wings and lifted from the ground, slipping through the air, until he fetched up against the middle of his own house, clinging to the window-sill of a bedroom.

Something screamed inside, and there was a clatter as someone fled downstairs.

At once Aldect was outside, shouting and asking what was going on. Antar turned to see who it was, and lost his hold, falling down in the path almost on top of Aldect. Maray was out next, thinking that the house was about to fall, that the volcano had started again and sent something worse than ash this time. She had Roslin in her arms.

Antar was jumping up and down, shouting in his turn, and no one knew what he was, much less who. They took him for some strange bird without a head. Maray looked from Antar to Roslin, bewildered because now Antar's hair was so long he was like a twin to his sister.

All at once they knew. Maray sat down. Roslin burst into tears. She would have liked a bird as well, she said, so Antar himself was not enough.

"Antar," said Aldect. "Is it you?"

"Gadar," said Antar. "I mean Antar. I have been with the eagles. One of them has come back with me. Garak, where are you?" He had to repeat it in the eagle language, while Maray and Roslin danced round him hugging him and picking at his feathers, not knowing what was true and what was not.

Garak came down from the roof, where he was dancing from one foot to the other, thinking something was comical. He would not come very near at all, expecting his feathers to be damaged. Antar had to go to him, knowing what he must do. They bowed to each other.

Antar scratched Garak's neck for the last time, and Garak scratched Antar's for the first time.

"Goodbye, goose," he said. "Come to the mountains and we shall be there. You are egg-mother to the Great Eagle, do not forget, and egg-brother to all eagles."

"Oh Garak," said Antar, "I love you."

Garak walked backwards, embarrassed, blinking his eyes as birds do, then fled because people were coming from houses and people are danger.

Maray, being a human mother, pulled Antar's clothes from him, feathers and all, and washed him in the tub in front of the fire. Her tears of happiness made the water salty.

"You will never be clean," she said. "I do not care."

"Goose?" said Aldect, because Antar was telling them everything. "Didn't they mean gander?"

"Raw meat?" said Roslin, wrinkling her nose.

Aren't people big and thick? thought Antar.

Then he was called to look at the church, where the other two sentinels were hanging in the air above the golden cross, throwing something from one to the other, talon to talon.

With a last cry one of them put this thing on the cross, and the pair of them flew away.

"My sentinels," said Antar. "I know them. But I do not know what they have done."

For a long time the thing on the cross did not move. Then below it the church clock chimed, and the thing woke up, yawned, stood up, stretched itself. It looked down, and started to call for help.

It was Antar's kitten. The sentinels had brought it so gently and carefully, and put it on the nearest place they dared come to, carrying it while it still slept; and had managed not to eat it on the journey from the mountains.

Antar, still wrapped in a towel, ran across to the church, and without thinking about it at all ran up a corner of the stonework, past the dream holes, to the spire, climbed up the lead, looped himself round the ball, and brought the kitten down.

He called it Garak. Between them they knew how he had been an egg-mother, but no one else understood.

Many years later, in the mountains, an aging bird came down to him when he called its name, and they talked of times known to both of them, far off, like a dream. But Kekayakan did not come to Antar.

"All young things leave home," said Garak. "It is as it should be. But he sends this to be your mark." And a golden feather (because all Great Eagles are golden in their prime) became Antar's sign in the world.

ABOUT THE AUTHOR

William Mayne completed a first novel at the age of sixteen and decided that writing would be his career. Since his first work for children was published in 1953, he has gained a prestigious reputation as an author of fiction and has written over sixty books. His novels include *A Grass Rope,* for which he won the Carnegie Medal, *Drift, All the King's Men,* and, most recently from Delacorte Press, *Gideon Ahoy!*

William Mayne lives in a small cottage in the Yorkshire dales.

J FIC Mayne
Mayne, William
Antar and the eagles.   13.95

J FIC Mayne
Mayne, William   172 6530
Antar and the eagles.   13.95

9/90

Farmingdale Public Library

Farmingdale, L.I., New York

Phone: CHapel 9-9090

*An Early Library Bird
Gathers No Fines*

WITHDRAWN FA